Public Relations Crisis Communication

This book explores the definition, nature and context of public relations crises; it also examines and defines the main elements of public relations crises and positions it in the context of the current communication sphere.

Public Relations Crisis Communication: A New Model investigates existing group communication theories, including organizational culture, critical theory of organizations, media ecology, public rhetoric, and cross-cultural communication theory to establish their relevance in the context of the new model of public relations crisis. Key concepts from existing public relations crisis theory are also discussed and validated in order to establish prevailing thought. Through a case study of Malaysia Airlines MH370, involving a textual analyses of press communications on the Malaysia Airlines website, this book scrutinises prevailing theory and definitions. Most valuably, this book proposes a new definition and model of public relations crisis, alongside a suggested extension to existing crisis communication theory in the form of a hierarchy of publics to be addressed during crises. This will help to address divergent publics with differing priorities in public relations crisis communication.

This book is of interest to students, teachers, researchers and practitioners of public relations, communication, media and marketing, as well as professionals in the aviation industry and international relations.

Lisa Anderson-Meli is a public relations professional with extensive experience in the aviation industry. She has a Masters in media and communication with specialisation in public relations.

Swapna Koshy is an award-winning professor and researcher who has published books and articles on communication. Dr Koshy's research focuses on media, marketing and business communication and the socio-cultural impact of new and traditional media.

Routledge Focus on Business and Management

The fields of business and management have grown exponentially as areas of research and education. This growth presents challenges for readers trying to keep up with the latest important insights. Routledge Focus on Business and Management presents small books on big topics and how they intersect with the world of business research.

Individually, each title in the series provides coverage of a key academic topic, whilst collectively, the series forms a comprehensive collection across the business disciplines.

Employment Relations and Ethnic Minority Enterprise
An Ethnography of Chinese Restaurants in the UK
Xisi Li

Women, Work and Migration
Nursing in Australia
Diane van den Broek and Dimitria Groutsis

Distributed Leadership and Digital Innovation
The Argument for Couple Leadership
Caterina Maniscalco

Public Relations Crisis Communication
A New Model
Lisa Anderson-Meli and Swapna Koshy

For more information about this series, please visit: www.routledge.com/Routledge-Focus-on-Business-and-Management/book-series/FBM

Public Relations Crisis Communication

A New Model

Lisa Anderson-Meli and Swapna Koshy

Routledge
Taylor & Francis Group

LONDON AND NEW YORK

First published 2020
by Routledge
2 Park Square, Milton Park, Abingdon, Oxon OX14 4RN

and by Routledge
52 Vanderbilt Avenue, New York, NY 10017

Routledge is an imprint of the Taylor & Francis Group, an informa business

British Library Cataloguing-in-Publication Data
A catalogue record for this book is available from the British Library

Library of Congress Cataloging-in-Publication Data
Names: Anderson-Meli, Lisa, author. | Koshy, Swapna, author.
Title: Public relations crisis communication: a new model /
Lisa Anderson-Meli and Swapna Koshy.
Description: First Edition. | New York: Routledge, 2020. |
Series: Routledge focus on business & management |
Includes bibliographical references and index.
Identifiers: LCCN 2019046804 (print) | LCCN 2019046805 (ebook) |
Subjects: LCSH: Public relations. | Corporate culture. | Communication.
Classification: LCC HD59 .A53 2020 (print) | LCC HD59 (ebook) |
DDC 659.2—dc23
LC record available at https://lccn.loc.gov/2019046804
LC ebook record available at https://lccn.loc.gov/2019046805

ISBN: 978-0-367-25429-2 (hbk)
ISBN: 978-0-429-28776-3 (ebk)

Typeset in Times New Roman
by codeMantra

MIX
Paper from
responsible sources
FSC
www.fsc.org   FSC™ C013985

Printed in the United Kingdom
by Henry Ling Limited

Contents

Foreword

How public relations and crisis communication fit in the continuum between academic disciplines and operational public relations and crisis communication, as practised by public relations (PR) agencies, corporations and consultants, is discussed in the first part of this useful guide by Lisa Anderson Meli and Dr Swapna Koshy.

The authors cite various definitions of public relations, communication and crisis communication. In covering this vast ground, they note that in the academic discipline and the corporate setting, public relations and communication are often assigned to various areas, sometimes lumped and sometimes separated, under communication, marketing, branding or indeed management, among currently popular terms.

Regardless of who in a corporation or governing body associated with a crisis is responsible for crisis communication, there are too many well-known incidents of crisis communication that were done badly, meaning that the crisis trailed the reputation of the responsible body for years after it had allegedly been settled.

The BP oil spill on April 20, 2010, resulted from an explosion on the Deepwater Horizon platform in the Gulf of Mexico. Given that 11 workers on the platform died, and environmental damage shocked the economies of fishermen and localities along the U.S. part of the Gulf, it was a difficult situation that required careful crisis communication. Instead, it became a defining example of how crisis communication can go wrong.

Workers died; livelihoods were lost. Someone at BP decided it wasn't necessary for CEO Tony Hayward to return from vacation because the corporate story could be told by company spokespersons. What no one realised at BP was that during a crisis, the boss has to be visible to accept responsibility and to apologise. Hayward returned some days later to take over communication, but the damage had been done. BP had failed to demonstrate sufficiently its concern about the situation.

In addition, in the U.S., this was a company still identified with Britain (BP was formed in 1998 from the American Amoco and British Petroleum) polluting the Gulf, affecting thousands of residents along the coastal U.S., and Hayward, when he was finally heard in public, spoke with a marked posh British accent. Americans generally like Britain and British accents, from cockney to Oxbridge, but not in this case. They listened to Hayward and heard a snooty-sounding foreigner not being humble enough. Hayward resigned from his position in July 2010, three months after the oil spill, a casualty of awful crisis communication.

That lesson, that the CEO or whoever is the boss must appear in public to accept responsibility and to apologise, has been learned in some cases but not always. As Anderson-Meli and Koshy point out, one of the classic organisational responses to a crisis is to ignore it – even after all that has been learned about crisis communication after years of academic studies and practical experience. If we don't say anything, no one will notice, and the problem will go away. Maybe that worked in the past. In our world, it cannot. Damaging photos and videos will appear almost immediately. Digital tools, from phones to laptops, make everything and every place accessible.

This weekend as I write this foreword in South Florida, we have been preparing for the arrival of Hurricane Dorian. Constant updates from weather services and the National Hurricane Center have charted Dorian's progress from Category 1 to Category 5 and its passage through the western Atlantic Ocean. We have stocked up on water and other supplies in case of a direct hit on our communities, although it looks now that Dorian is heading north and may attack northern coasts of Florida, Georgia, and the Carolinas.

The reason to mention Hurricane Dorian in terms of crisis communication is that five days ago, President Donald Trump was set to visit Poland, an important North Atlantic Treaty Organization(NATO) ally, to commemorate the start of the Second World War with the Nazi invasion of Poland on September 1, 1939. The President cancelled that trip at the last minute in order to remain in the White House to manage federal response to the hurricane.

One might argue that his being in the U.S. or abroad makes no difference to victims of the hurricane. However, Americans – and much of the world – have come to expect that the chief/boss/president/CEO will be at hand during a serious crisis – if not to accept responsibility or apologise, specifically to demonstrate caring and involvement. That cannot be done from another country. All news media would lead with the headline 'President Trump in Poland as Dorian Hits U.S. East Coast'. Social media would explode with the same message.

Clearly, crisis communication has become a separate area with its own rules. Despite the academic literature and the corporate experience, there is no final agreement on what constitutes crisis communication and how it is deployed during a crisis. The authors tackle the important definitions of what constitutes a crisis and how crisis communication may be managed to arrive at the overriding concern of this study: determining the publics or stakeholders in a crisis and deciding which are the most important.

Curiously, this aspect of crisis communication has not been considered by academics up to now. What the authors call the hierarchy of publics in a crisis is what they explore in detail in *A Hierarchy of Crisis Publics: A New Dimension to Public Relations Crisis Communication Theory*.

It is easy for academics and practitioners to list categories of stakeholders in any crisis: shareholders, suppliers, clients, local communities, national and international individuals and groups, along with politicians, think tanks and nonprofits, among others. But not all figure into every crisis because every crisis has its unique aspects. The task for those who have to manage crisis communication is to target the most important publics and create messages for them first.

Anderson-Meli and Koshy point out that the state of media today makes it difficult to capture key audiences or publics in time. It has been said – as they repeat – that there is a "golden hour" from the moment the existence of a crisis is recognised. In that hour, the path of communication must be launched.

Formerly, news agencies were usually the first to identify a crisis in one or two lines of headline text. Daily newspapers had a deadline in the evening and would deliver the first more extensive description of a crisis the following day. News magazines were even slower, of course, although they would provide more background and context with their later deadlines. Broadcast television and radio fell somewhere in between, with video and sound highlights early but background and context much later, if they had not veered away to cover the next crisis.

That kind of relative leisure, allowing for information to be gathered, spokespeople to be found and prepared, and a timeline of releases and updates to be set, is gone with digital media. The horrific explosion at the Union Carbide pesticide plant in Bhopal, India, that killed at least 4,000 people in early December 1984 would have been seen in photos and eyewitness interviews within minutes of the explosion – had it happened in our digital everyone-is-an-eyewitness era.

By the time the owners of the factory began to supply information to news media, a great deal of information would already be on the

Internet because today a transmission truck is not necessary to provide stills, sound and video from most places in the world. A smartphone is enough. Developing countries have some of the highest rates of penetration of smartphones, so it is no longer feasible to set times for when information is released. It has to happen as soon as possible.

During the golden hour, those in charge and ultimately responsible for the crisis, be they a government or a corporation, must begin informing the most important key public first, with others, in turn, following after that. For President Trump this week, the most important public is Americans in South Atlantic states and throughout the country. To speak to fellow citizens, he is willing to risk the disappointment of the second-most important public – those in Poland waiting for him to reinforce the military guarantee of NATO.

To demonstrate what was done in an actual acute crisis in 2014, the authors focus the second part of their book on the case study of the disappearance of Malaysia Airlines MH370. They evaluate what was done and not done in releasing information, and reflect on opportunities missed in terms of the hierarchy of publics addressed.

The disappearance of any aircraft carrying 239 passengers and crew anywhere is an enormous tragedy for numerous publics, but in this specific case, the tragedy was compounded by the ownership of the airline, the departure airport, the arrival airport MH370 never reached and the history of the primary publics. All this is detailed in this excellent study that creates a new category within crisis communication and makes the convincing case for its importance. Public relations and crisis communication students, academics and practitioners will need to reckon with the findings of Anderson-Meli and Koshy the next time they study, teach or manage a crisis.

Dr Alma Kadragic
President
Alcat Communications International LLC

Dr Alma Kadragic has been a journalist, researcher, media specialist and entrepreneur in the U.S., Europe and the Middle East. Her career includes a 16-year stint with ABC News in New York, Washington D.C., London and Warsaw as writer, producer and bureau chief. She co-founded Poland's first PR association and served as its first president. In 2013 she was awarded the Officer's Cross for Service by the President of Poland for her journalistic work.

Kadragic's publications include two books: *Public Relations or Promoting Reputations* (1997, 1998), the first PR handbook in Polish, and *Globalization and Human Rights* (2006).

Dr Kadragic has served on many boards, including American Women in Radio and Television (President, New York City, Orlando chapters), Middle East PR Association, American Chamber of Commerce in Poland, Fulbright Commission in Poland, National Association of Women Business Owners (President, Miami chapter) and Entrepreneur Advisory Board of the Disney/SBA National Entrepreneur Center.

Introduction

Over the last century the world has become increasingly closer and infinitely more accessible. The growth and availability of new and ubiquitous means of communication and the parallel progression of international travel through commercial airlines have facilitated global connectivity. It is also important to recognise that there have been differences in the rate of change the world has experienced with the speed of development of the last decade eclipsing that of the last century. The pace at which this has occurred has inspired commentators to refer to the period as the Fourth Industrial Revolution given the rapidly emerging technologies promoted by digitisation and artificial intelligence. Clearly the world and its population are experiencing a period of accelerated transformation, which shows no signs of abating as we struggle to keep pace with developments in data and connectivity.

The Fourth industrial revolution and the novel means of communication it has generated have given rise to new challenges in the sphere of communication, especially crisis communication. The changes in communication technology and the speed of message traffic have impacted the way in which we communicate in a crisis. Nearly half of the world's population, approximately 4.4 billion people, now use the internet, with most countries experiencing exponential growth (World Internet Usage and Population Statistics 2019). Individuals and collective entities such as Governments, Organisations, Interest Groups, Corporations and others are adding to the overwhelming amount of data available. In 2018 Forbes revealed that we were producing over 2.5 quintillion bytes of data a day (Marr, 2018). The volume of information is escalating in conjunction with connectivity, convenience and convergence. The ability to control messages both in terms of content and distribution is a futile exercise. Negativity in news reporting has increased negativity bias where the bad-news sticks and consumers respond more to it (Leetaru, 2016). Given the possibility of negativity bias, the revolution in communication with its associated unpredictability is bound to have repercussions for the field of public relations crisis communications.

The ability of an organisation to control the information being disseminated, or to control the conversations taking place around it, has diminished, and this is more glaring when the news is negative. While crisis communication remains the 'elephant in the room', for many organisations, its importance cannot be overstated. It is during a crisis that an organisation's communication comes under increased scrutiny. Thus, a study of crisis communication provides an ideal crucible in which to explore existing theory and how it responds to the demands of the new communication status quo. Further, it is the propensity for organisations and their designated representatives to still get it incredulously wrong, after decades of theoretical development and practice in crisis communication, that warrants ongoing investigation.

Before engaging in the examination of existing theory it is important to establish the function of public relations as an academic discipline and vocational practice. Related definitions also have to be established along with validating the changes to speed, volume and channels of communication engaged in public relations crisis communication in the post-evolutionary era of communication technology.

Despite the debate over the validity of Public Relations as a scholarly discipline (Botan & Hazelton, 2006) it is worth noting that crisis communication seems to have found its identity within the remit of Public Relations. While this is a relatively recent phenomenon, and some communication specialists question this allocation, it is worth noting Caroline Black's (2014) observation that public relations always necessitates communication, while communication is not always public relations.

Noting the above it is also essential to understand the disciplines that co-relate to and overlap public relations, as the vocational practice is variably assigned to corporate communications, marketing communications or public engagement, amongst others. Acknowledging this, the primary function of public relations and its distinction from other forms of communication, particularly with respect to crisis communication, needs to be ascertained.

A key concept of this book, and indeed of the discipline, is the conception and perception of publics, or stakeholders as they are sometimes referred to. Interestingly this has not been adequately explored in relation to public relations crisis communication. For example, there has been no attempt to define the publics in a crisis or to establish if different publics are of equal importance in a crisis. How an organisation communicates with publics in a crisis; if it should be the same for every public and whether publics react or respond in homogenous patterns to a crisis need to be investigated. This raises the proposition of a hierarchy of crisis publics and the necessity to ascertain whether the creation of such a hierarchy would positively impact public relations crisis communication.

To date, theories of public relations crisis communication have focused mainly on the organisational response and the event itself. However, understanding the relationship of various publics to an event and subsequent crisis may provide a deeper and more accurate assessment of a public's attribution of responsibility. If this can be achieved it is likely to facilitate a more precise organisational response thereby improving the efficiency and success of crisis communications.

Introducing the concept of a hierarchy of crisis publics as a possible extension to existing theory will be carried out by examining the case of Malaysian Airlines MH370. The international aviation industry is a worthy starting point because of the specificity of events, resulting severe crises, multiplicity of publics, international nature and interest of global community.

1 Public relations crisis communication

Developing a conceptual framework

Defining public relations

Ever since Edward L. Bernays in *Crystallizing Public Opinion* (1923) substituted 'propaganda' with the more positive term 'Public Relations' coined by Thomas Jefferson (Davis cited in Gonçalves, 2014, p. 100) a multitude of definitions and interpretations of the term have been generated. These include Aristotle's early work on rhetoric to the nineteenth-century war-related propaganda and more recently the professionalisation of public relations as a management function.

The Public Relations Society of America (PRSA) surveyed its members from 2011 to 2012 with the aim of updating their 1982 definition of what constituted public relations. The definition that was agreed upon is "public relations is about influencing, engaging and building a relationship with key stakeholders across a myriad of platforms in order to shape and frame the public perception of an organization" (PRSA, 2019).

Regardless of whether public relations is viewed as an activity, profession and/or scholarly pursuit, and whether it is defined as positive, normative or pejorative, it ultimately concerns itself with the specific relationship between an organisation (in all its guises) and its publics (in all their forms). While this may initially appear tautological these relationships are not static, and it is the manifestations and machinations of organisational-public relationships that often engender debate. Notwithstanding this it is imperative that the operational negotiations surrounding public relations do not detract from its core principle; that is, the 'doing' of public relations should not mire a definition of what public relations 'is'. It is essential to note that the activity of public relations necessitates communication, the two are inexorably linked; it is through communication that relationships transpire. Therefore, we can establish the definition of public relations, at its most basic level, as **the manifestation (communication) of the relationships between an organisation and its publics.**

Public relations crisis explained

As the focus of this book is public relations crisis communication it is also necessary to define public relations crisis, the associated terminology of crisis management and the various actors or elements involved.

It is ironic that the word crisis is derived from the Greek 'krisis' meaning decision or judgement (Maditinos & Vassiliadis, 2008). The considerations an organisation is confronted with during a public relations crisis include: deciding what to say, if anything; when to say it; who to say it to; and, with today's communication landscape, how to say it. These decisions are the key to successful public relations crisis communication and have been visited and revisited by various scholars, public relations practitioners and those that advise them in order to determine what is variously described as best practice. However, as with the definition of public relations the above questions are concerned with the 'doing' of public relations crisis communications and not essentially what public relations crisis 'is'.

A starting point for the definition of public relations crisis is Fink's observation that "a crisis occurs when an event increases in intensity, falls under the scrutiny of the news, media or government, interferes with normal business opportunities, devalues a positive public image, and has an adverse effect on a business' 'bottom line'" (Fink cited in Butterick, 2011, p. 62). Fearn-Banks (2011, p. 2) stresses on the distinction between a crisis and a problem – a crisis disturbs the regular flow of business and therefore cannot be deemed a 'normal' part of day-to-day operations. Faulkner cites Selbst's definition of a crisis as

> any action or failure to act that interferes with an [organisation's] on-going functions, the acceptable attainment of its objectives, its viability or survival, or that has a detrimental personal effect as perceived by the majority of its employees, clients or constituents.
> Selbst 1978 cited in Faulkner, 2001, p. 136

Interestingly, Anthonissen (2012) highlights the involvement of the media, who, he argues, exaggerate and publicise incidents within hours of their occurrence.

Some theorists identify unpredictability as a feature of crises; hence, 'crisis planning' would be an oxymoron (Coombs, 2012). Brown refers to probabilism, reassurance and risk management. However, when discussing predictability, he accepts Coombs exclusion of natural disasters as statistical outliers, noting the assumption that a human crisis can be "discovered, prevented, contained, controlled" is a dubious one (Brown, 2015, p. 22). It is inaccurate to view all events as completely unpredictable given the very rationale for crisis management is based on a degree of inevitability. While it is agreed that there can be an element of 'surprise', for example, predicting when an event will occur may not be possible, the justification for crisis management relies on preparedness. The argument follows that if a crisis is discoverable it can be preventable; if it is not preventable, it can be controlled or minimised; if it cannot be controlled, it can be resolved. The use of communication to prevent, minimise, control and resolve crises is the cornerstone of public relations crisis management.

Though all the definitions discussed earlier have elements of validity their focus is narrow and therefore problematic for public relations professionals who seek to effectively quantify what constitutes a public relations crisis. Nonetheless, from various definitions it is possible to determine important rudiments that provide the basis for a workable definition. From Fink's (2011) definition it is clear that there are multiple factors that can lead to a crisis, from Norton's (2013) that it is necessarily negative, from Fearn-Banks' (2011) that it is an a-typical occurrence, from Selbst's (1978 cited in Faulkner, 2001) that it must impact the organisation and its publics and from Anthonissen's (2012) that it occurs in the public arena.

Heath's (2012) work catalogues over 20 definitions highlighting the emphasis on various aspects of crises. He agrees with Coombs' observations that "if stakeholders believe there is a crisis, the organisation is in crisis unless it can successfully persuade stakeholders it is not" (Coombs, 2012; p. 6). This explanation of crisis is an improvement on previous attempts as it refers to stakeholders. However, it does not address the origin of stakeholder perceptions or the provocations of crises, although whether these are significant is questionable.

Related to the aforementioned provocations of crises there is also a tendency amongst theorists to view various events, incidents, issues and crises as synonymous; however, this is confusing. Faulkner's (2001) delineation of crisis and disaster where the latter is defined as being inflicted on an organisation is reminiscent of Anthonissen's (2012) typology of events and Ulmer et al.'s (2015) division of intentional and unintentional crises. These descriptions and classifications do not assist in terms of defining a public relations crisis but aid in describing the provocations.

An organisation is confronted daily by events (or incidents) that have the potential to become issues or crises. Regardless of the type of events/incidents they are not the same as an organisational issue or crisis though interrelated. If every event or incident was defined as a crisis, organisations would be paralysed and constantly engaging in crisis communication.

Building upon the earlier definitions of public relations crises an improved explanation of what a public relations crisis 'is' has been proposed below:

> A public relations crisis is triggered by an event, issue or incident and is the critical breakdown of relationship between an organisation and one (or more) of its publics, threatening the organisation's existence and warranting an organisational response.

Considering Coombs' (2012) addition of stakeholders in the definition of crisis communication it must be noted that the relationship breakdown is perceived by the concerned public and becomes evident via negative connections or communications. By affirming Coombs' focus on the public's perception of crisis as a definitional requirement the importance of publics can be ascertained.

It is essential to set these relationships in the context of the new communication status quo, which means they no longer exist in isolation. The relationships between an organisation and its publics are no longer distinct or homogenous. Due to the very nature of the new communication sphere, they are increasingly interrelated. This relational convergence is evidenced in the communication domain where one relationship schism can trigger another in an ongoing cycle.

In an attempt to generate a workable definition of public relations crises the distinction between event, issue, incident and crisis is illustrated in Figure 1.1. The 'events' or 'incidents' listed below, while not definitive, have been divided into internal or external, but could also be described according to the degree of human involvement. What is important to note about the figure is that the incident or event is not the issue or the crisis, it merely constitutes a potential trigger.

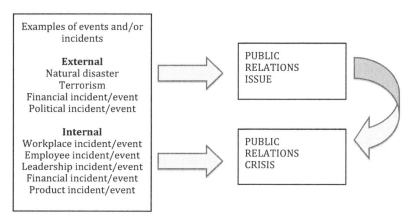

Figure 1.1 Event/incident, issue and crisis.

Contextualising public relations crises

Given the above definition it is now necessary to examine the contextualisation of crises and the method scholars and commentators have used to frame crises in order to aid understanding and formulate theory.

The most commonly used contextualisation is the application of crisis stages. Norton (2013) identifies three stages of crisis management: pre-crisis, crisis response and post-crisis evaluation. Coombs (2012) agrees with this referring to the second stage simply as crisis, while Griffin (2014) identifies five stages: prediction, prevention, preparation, resolution and recovery. This is similar to Fearn-Banks' (2011) five stages of detection, prevention/preparation, containment, recovery and learning, which combines stages two and three of Griffins and adds learning as the fifth and final stage. It is important to note that this method of contextualisation has generated great criticism. Frandsen and Johansen (2011) critique the staged approach as too procedural pointing out that it does not consider overlapping or multiple crises occurring at the same time. However, applying a procedural approach does not exclude multiplicity; it simply provides a framework for managing the variables at differing points in a crisis timeline. Further, as each stage informs the proceeding one, the stages are necessarily interrelated and therefore overlap.

Other commentators overlay the above with a classification of crisis. For example, Maditinos and Vassiliadis (2008) cite Parson's categorisation of immediate, emerging and sustained crisis as well as Karagiannis' classification of crises according to human involvement, be it direct, indirect or no human involvement. Also included is Sausmarez who divides crises according to whether they are natural or man-made. However, if we accept that the event or incident is a potential crises trigger then Karagiannis and Sausmarez are offering event descriptions rather than crises contextualisation. Further, if it is acknowledged that a public relations crisis is the acute relationship schism between an organisation and one or more of its publics (incorporating the severity of possible outcomes noted in the earlier definition) then it follows that public relations crises have an inherent human factor.

However, Parson's (cited in Maditinos and Vassiliadis, 2008) categorisation of immediate, emerging and sustained crises is relevant particularly in relation to this book's definition as illustrated in Figure 1.1. That is, an immediate crisis can be seen to occur when the incident/event causes an immediate acute relationship schism. An emerging crisis can be seen as a link between a public relations issue and a public relations crisis, in that a crisis emerges from poor public relations issue management. Finally, a sustained crisis refers to poor public relations crisis management (communication) where the organisation is unsuccessful in communicating *through* the crisis and becomes mired in constant crisis communication. The salient point is the human involvement at each point in the model as evidenced by Figure 1.2.

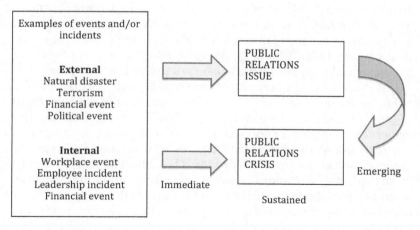

Figure 1.2 Immediate, emerging and sustained crisis.

It is therefore logical that the 'resolution' phase or 'crisis' phase is critical in determining a positive outcome and avoiding a sustained crisis. Pearson et al. (1997) refer to the damage containment phase as garnering the most investment by organisations. The term 'containment' should be approached with caution given its potential for relativity and inaccuracy. Griffin's (2014) notion of resolution where relationship reparation is the priority is a more apposite submission. During this resolution phase organisational communication is most heavily scrutinised, with the comportment of communication viewed as indicative of the organisation. As referred to earlier in this chapter, four key factors stand out in the response phase: what to say, when to say it, how to say it and who to say it to – this is the sum total of an organisation's crisis communication.

From the suggested definition of public relations crisis, it is obvious that particular elements are omnipresent: the event, the organisation, the public (or publics) involved and the communication sphere, where interaction between the organisation and their publics takes place. In order to understand the environment of public relations crises all of these elements must also be defined in order to establish how they interact and impact public relations crises.

The difference between events, incidents, issues and crises

While the complexity and nature of events and incidents is not the focus of this book it is clear that in the context of this discussion references to events or incidents simply denote an occurrence that takes place at a certain time and or place that has the potential to impact an organisation, the organisation's publics and the relationships that exist between them. It must be remembered, however, that these impacts can lead to public relations issues or public relations crises.

It is essential to distinguish between a public relations issue and a public relations crisis, and this has been graphically represented in Figures 1.1 and 1.2. The distinction is clear by virtue of the severity and potential impact a public relations crisis has on an organisation's relationships. A crisis necessarily requires 'all hands on deck' to ensure the relationships under threat survive. The critical factor is the severity so that a public relations crisis requires an organisational response, whereas a public relations issue in spite of the challenge it presents for an organisation can be managed by an individual department or team. Coombs (2012) also acknowledges this distinction by observing that the term 'crisis' should be reserved for serious events.

It is worthwhile noting a further clarification of the term 'organisational response' in the context of public relations crises. Organisations continually respond to events and/or incidents. However, these responses are not necessarily public relations crisis responses. Organisational responses to events or incidents can be contextualised by the absence, or presence, of an acute relationship schism, and its presence necessitates public relations crisis communication.

The organisation defined

Organisational type is a factor influencing a specific organisation's public relations crisis communication. The organisation has remained a central focus of both public relations crisis communication research and practice, particularly given its focal point in the dissemination of public relations. Therefore, a detailed categorisation of organisations could serve to add insight into the complexities of public relations crisis communication and potentially offer a basis for an improvement in understanding its nuances and, in turn, improving outcomes.

Smith (2013) defines organisations as broadly being either not-for-profit or profit-making entities while noting the myriad variants on either side of this categorisation. However, regardless of whether an organisation is defined as profit making or not, they are always engaged in communication with their publics. Apart from the economic rationale of an organisation and its associated structures, all of which warrant further investigation in relation to public relations crisis communication, it is the fact that an organisation does not exist in isolation that is most relevant for this discussion.

Organisations, defined as collective entities, exist in relation to other entities, namely publics, and these relationships manifest in the communication sphere. It is this relationship that is key for this study of public relations crisis communication, and therefore the two remaining elements to define are publics and the communication sphere.

An organisation's relationship to its publics is neither static nor fixed. The relationship can be transient, the public can be transitional and, as Gordon (2011) argues, organisations themselves can constitute a public.

Who are Publics?

The term 'Public' is a contentious one within public relations. For example, Smith (2013) delineates between publics, markets, audiences and stakeholders. While these divisions present valuable distinctions in terms of the nature of the relationships these entities have with or to an organisation, all are relational publics of an organisation. Therefore, while these terms contextualise publics according to their relationship, they do not necessarily provide a fundamental definition or clarification. Smith (2013) proceeds to divide publics into four categories: customers, producers, enablers and limiters. However, one could argue, based on his earlier classification, that customers and producers belong to the market grouping as well as or as opposed to the public grouping. This highlights the potential for confusion when defining through contextualisation. This is not to say that contextualisation lacks relevance but definition and contextualisation are separate functions. A functional definition facilitates effective contextualisation. This is not dissimilar to the complexity encountered with distinguishing events, issues and crises.

Gregory (2012) highlights Esman's (1972) use of linkages to define the publics an organisation can develop relationships with. Publics are defined by their relationship to the organisation be it normative, functional, enabling or diffused. Gordon (2011) cites Grunig and Hunt's (1984) observation that publics "are transient in how and when they exist". Gordon (2011) also refers to Leitch and Neilson's (2001) assertion that publics are created and recreated as the people that constitutes publics interpret and act upon messages. Leitch and Neilson's (2001) observation is particularly relevant in the current communication sphere given the constant multiple messaging activities of the various entities present.

From the above it is clear that publics constitute multiple transformative groupings, with various relationships with an organisation. Smith (2013) makes a significant observation in terms of intercessory publics, which he defines as having independent relationship with an organisation's publics outside of the organisation's control. These external relationships undoubtedly create a significant layer of complication for an organisation. While this is valuable there needs to be a distinction in the level of intercession such that it extends beyond the interrelational public relationships that exist in communication today.

Applying Smith's (2013) concept of the intercessory public and the above contingency it is clear that the media constitutes a primary example of an intercessory public. Media, in all its forms, interposes between an organisation and its publics. However, with the advent of digital media, this interruption has become more prevalent and progressively more volatile facilitating a level of intercession not previously possible.

The digital landscape is diverse and growing, and nearly every conventional media format is represented on at least one social platform.

Conventional media is an exceptional intercessory public in that it actively seeks content from other publics. The changed status quo of the communication sphere warrants that reference be made to the changes that digital media have imposed on the news cycle. The resultant demand for content has progressively increased affecting the behaviour of media as an intercessory public.

If a thorough understanding of an organisation's publics is essential for routine communication, it is indispensable for public relations crisis communication given the intense scrutiny of communication between an organisation and its publics during a crisis. Crisis communication is arguably the primary tool for crisis management as it helps to measure an organisation's ability to manage a crisis and, in turn, acts as a predictor of an organisation's success in ensuring the survival of its relationships.

The relationship between an organisation and its publics has been discussed in absolute terms. However, this relationship can be perceived differently by both the organisation and its publics. It can be formal or informal, real or abstract, positive or negative, but it is the perceived connection that is relevant, particularly from a public's perspective, which can differ markedly from that of the organisation.

These connections symbolising the relationship manifest via messages in the communication sphere. The nature of the connection between an organisation and its publics is realised here, and changes in these connections or relationships are also evident. As Griffin (2012, p. 6) notes, "communication is a relational process not only because it takes place between people but also because it affects the nature of the connections among those people". Now that the definition of public relations has been established it is imperative that the communication sphere also is defined and contextualised.

Delineating the communication sphere

The communication sphere of today is not only the arena where messages are coded, sent, received, decoded and shared but also the space where the relationships between an organisation and its publics are realised. It is essential to reiterate that this sphere is not made up of a set of neat singular pathways of communication between an organisation and its publics but a congested set of highways and byways constantly criss-crossing each other. This maze of communication generates a continual stream of traffic where various messages are relentlessly dispatched, received and relayed between public to public, organisation to public and public to organisation. The complexity for an organisation in the communication sphere today is that they have relatively little control (if any) over the information that is generated by their publics.

Within the communication sphere various publics (static, transitory and transformational) interact with each other. The publics relevant for this discussion are mainly the publics the organisation has a relationship with and intercessory publics who actively seek to intrude.

While considering the media as a primary intercessory public it is important to note that journalists (and other media personnel) are now under increasing pressure to create more content with less resources. Digital media has not only altered the volume of media as Bucy and Holbert (2011) note, but it has also fundamentally altered how we consume media (Silvia & Anzur, 2011). The digital platform has created a news beast with an insatiable appetite, and this has resulted in shorter deadlines and increased competition, resulting in a continual search for new sources of information, including that discharged via social media.

There is another aspect to the constant demand for content and that is the perpetuation of news. The lengthening of a story's shelf life, by whatever means, can be considered a potential saving of resources, as it is one less 'new' piece of content that needs to be created in order to meet volume expectations. A straightforward way to achieve this is to seek multiple perspectives of the same event/incident, that is, to seek input from various publics on any given event. Media commentators would argue that a thorough investigation adds value to news stories and not just creates bulk.

The communication sphere post-digitisation operates constantly and ubiquitously, free of geographical boundaries. Messages flow continuously with limited restriction. This has been a relatively recent phenomenon and as such, has presented significant challenges for public relations practitioners, further exacerbated during crises. Norton (2013) notes that the power used to be firmly in the hands of professional communicators who had the budgets and resources to produce 'traditional media', but this is no longer the case given the advent of the internet and social media.

There is a massive amount of literature on the changing nature of the communication sphere stemming from the introduction of the internet and the consequential evolutionary shift in communication. Green (2010) highlights Yaxley's comments that the response to a crisis is never quick enough and therefore knowing how to intercept the message and give it a new focus gains importance. Gordon (2011) sums up some commonly agreed characteristics of the internet: it is low cost, reaches a mass audience and can distribute vast amounts of information which can be selected and compared simultaneously. The model proposed by Mcquail and Windahl (2015) sees groups of individuals as nodes connected by communication flows, with specific roles assigned to individuals according to their function within and across the nodes. The multiple web-like structure of the new communication sphere is an indication of the communication challenges facing organisations which intensifies during a crisis.

Relevant to this discussion is also the work of Frandsen and Johansen (2007) which claims that multiple voices are evident in the communication sphere. Coombs also notes that while there are multiple voices in a crisis only one message emanates from the organisation (Coombs & Holladay, 2014). Influencing the conversation when you are only one voice of many is the task organisations must embrace in the current communication sphere. Given the vast numbers of information sources or channels, it would seem logical to expect a dilution of messages. However, it is the connectivity of these new channels and the aforementioned consortiums of ownership that has created a convergence of media such that, as Gordon (2011) comments, organisations find themselves increasingly exposed as more information about them is both available and accessible.

While the lack of geographical boundaries raises issues about cross-cultural communication and dialogical communication it needs to be cautioned that the removal of boundaries does not automatically create homogenous publics (Kruckeberg, 1998). The need for nuanced culturally sensitive communication remains, particularly for an organisation engaging in crisis communication. However, it must be viewed in the context of the other variables, such as the event (was it international, domestic or localised), the organisation (does its operation span geographical boundaries and cultures) and the publics involved (are they culturally and geographically diverse).

It is not surprising that the communication sphere has garnered so much attention given the rapidity of change it has experienced in the last decade. The salient observation in terms of public relations crisis communication is that information moves quickly and independently of an organisation, thereby generating increased pressure on any organisational crisis communication response. There is effectively no margin for error as messages the organisation sends out are shared and re-distributed, magnifying and compounding mistakes or inconsistencies. In addition, there is minimal time to formulate and distribute these messages as the voracious demands of the 24-hour news cycle seek out information from any and all sources.

Establishing the parameters for the predominant elements involved in a public relations crisis: the organisation, the event or incident, the publics whose relationships with the organisation have been damaged by an event or its escalation and the new communication sphere where all communication is realised provides a basis for examining possible gaps in public relations crisis theory.

To understand how public relations crisis communication has changed in response to the new status quo we need to explore existing communication theories as well as those pertaining specifically to public relations crises as both concern themselves with interrelationships between the elements mentioned above. Relevance and redundancy need to be ascertained before the suggestion of a hierarchy of crisis publics can be made in order to improve outcomes for public relations crisis communication.

2 Contextualising theories of communication

In terms of public relations, particularly crisis communication, it is widely accepted that there is an increased visibility of communication in the crisis response phase. Therefore, it is necessary to explore relevant communication theories to test for applicability and relevance. Griffin (2012) identifies five key concepts in communication theory: messages, the creation of them, the interpretation of them, the response to them and the concept of communication as a relational process. He goes on to highlight Deetz's (1992) observation that all communication has two main priorities: efficacy and participation, with the former referring to *successful* communication, or more practically, messages reaching their intended destination, and the latter suggesting that these messages engender a response from their intended recipient. Interestingly, given what we have discussed about the current communication sphere and the notion of intercessory publics, a message (particularly during a crisis) may well reach audiences for which its content was unintended, and in doing so provoke unanticipated responses.

It is important to note the distinction between response or participation and reply. That is, publics can participate and respond to messages without necessarily *replying*. Green (2010) refers to the concept of spectators (as opposed to originators or contributors) in reference to social media. However, this could also be extended to online media and in fact, given current technology, communication in general. Spectators are participating by receiving, or viewing, messages or content, while contributors participate *and* respond to messages through feedback, either to the originator or another public, and originators generate the messages. Importantly, these are not static or isolated classifications as they overlap and transform according to the message. One could argue that contributors morph into originators when they engage in a response, particularly if it is directed to an entity other than that from whence it came. In addition, within any public there are representations of all three. An individual can inhabit all three at any given time depending on the circumstance. Conventional media (both digital and offline), as an intercessory public, seek out originators and contributors within each public (including the organisation) garnering diverse messages in an effort to meet content requirements. Given the significance of communication as the manifestation of relationships between publics or entities present in the current communication sphere it is essential to have a broad understanding of communication theory and where it fits into public relations crisis communication to assess how it has been impacted as a result of the discussed technological revolution.

An introduction to communication theory

Communication theory can be categorised into various groupings that broadly focus on inter-personal communication, group and/or public communication including organisational communication, mass communication and cross-cultural communication (Griffin, 2012).

Postmodernism contextualises much communication theory according to the premise that previous norms and assumptions are potentially no longer relevant or even applicable given the current communications sphere. Interestingly, in an era of social media, Griffin (2012) identifies some key beliefs of postmodernists: the importance of images and the media's functional ability to develop diverse styles and tastes, thereby creating a unique identity. This has significance for crisis communication in terms of digital technology, where images are easily transmitted online and being increasingly utilised. This is coupled with the convergence and accessibility of publics, including the media, through the digital platforms of the current communication sphere creating an increased opportunity for the media to intercept messages.

The effect of organisational culture on communication

Geertz and Pacanowsky (cited in Griffin, 2012) looked at the culture of organisations, arguing that they created their own narratives likened to webs of significance. These webs are created through communication, articulating the organisation's culture. This is important for crisis communication, as the organisation is a key element. These ideas can be linked to Benoit's image restoration theory (now often referred to as Image Repair theory) as the organisation utilises communication to alter its image and the perception of its culture (Coombs, 2006).

The culture of an organisation and its self-created narratives, including its predominant national culture and industry, may have an important bearing on crisis communication. It provides information on an organisation's *personality* (the combination of organisational image, vision, ethics and behaviour) as well as an indication of the events or incidents it may encounter.

Stanley Deetz's (1992) critical communication theory and his notion of corporate colonisation, where control is the overriding factor, sees communication as political as all information is sponsored and therefore value laden. Deetz argued against managerialism and corporate control advocating a stakeholder democracy approach to communication and decision-making. Deetz's participatory approach to communication is extremely relevant for the current communication sphere where it is increasingly challenging to achieve dominance or enact any meaningful control of messages during normal communication, let alone during a crisis. Deetz's stakeholder democracy is evocative of Grunig's symmetrical theory and stresses the significance of publics in communication. Therefore, a focus on publics as they function in crisis communication is essential for all phases of crisis efficacy and planning.

Media ecology

Marshall McLuhan's theory of media ecology is also relevant today. His oft-quoted axiom "the media is the message" (McLuhan, 1964 cited in Durham and Kellner, 2006) refers to the indivisibility of content from the media that carries it. However, a complete disregard for content is unwise given the already discussed negative bias of media and media consumption. Nonetheless, the relationship between medium and content cannot be denied as the former informs the latter. The nature of the technology circumscribes its use and therefore its content. As McLuhan argues, firearms cannot be characterised as neutral because their technology informs their use. That is, a firearm cannot be used to clean the house, its technology stipulates that it be used to fire bullets. More relevant for this discussion is the example of Twitter, which by virtue of its technology is now limited to 280 characters (up from its original 140), making brevity unavoidable. As will be seen in the examination of Malaysian Airlines MH370, the organisation's use of text messages was poorly received because the significance of the medium was not appreciated in terms of its impact on the message.

Griffin (2012, p. 322) defines media as "all human-invented technology that extends the range, speed or channels of communication" explaining that every medium encourages different habits and utilises different senses. McLuhan's four epochs of media, such as tribal, literacy, print and electronic, have greater legitimacy today as debate surrounds the inevitability of a fifth epoch. The rise of digitalisation and the supremacy of data, McLuhan argues, are creating a global village where electronic media is becoming increasingly personalised (McLuhan, 1964 cited in Griffin, 2012). The personalisation of content, not only according to the medium but also according to the intended (and perhaps unintended) recipient/s, provides a possible platform upon which a hierarchy of crisis publics can be constructed with a view to increased efficacy and participation. In addition, the notion of personalisation raises a discussion of cross-cultural communication, its presence and relevance for online media and importance for public relations crisis communication.

Theory of public rhetoric

Public Rhetoric Theory developed from Aristotle's writings on rhetoric in the fourth century BCE and focuses on the function of persuasion. Many theorists still perceive rhetoric as a central function of public relations. Aristotle viewed audiences as passive, an observation that has garnered much criticism and is a moot point even today (Griffin, 2012). Utilising Green's distinction between originators, contributors and spectators, essentially only the spectators could be regarded as passive and only if the assumption holds that receiving or viewing messages is synonymous with inertia or apathy. In addition, passivity can refer not just to action but also to belief systems. This intimates that publics are passive in their ideologies although this would appear to contradict the very premise of persuasion. Interestingly, combining McLuhan's digital personalisation and Aristotle's public rhetoric provides an insight into the ability of the current communication sphere to reinforce existing belief systems as opposed to challenging them.

Persuasion is a contentious issue for public relations with arguments supporting the preference of understanding over persuasion, intimating the negative connotations the concept of persuasion holds (Pfau & Wan, 2006). However, Pfau and Wan (2006) provide compelling arguments against this premise, not necessarily to refute understanding, but to defend persuasion. They acknowledge that persuasion is inherently manipulative, but contest that this alone does not render persuasion unethical. Further, a solution can be found in developing opposing lines of reasoning where a level of understanding is necessary for persuasion to be effective. This theory can also be linked to Benoit's theory, as organisational rhetoric is the vehicle of image restoration or repair. Further, it can also account for the limitations of image restoration as a predictor for effective crisis communication in that while the organisation remains focused on rhetoric and persuasion there is no understanding of the other elements in the crisis equation or the realities of the current communication sphere, thereby limiting efficacy.

Key themes from various communication theories are reflected in crisis communication theory. For example, the notion of credibility, audience adaptation, narrative and dialogue are all essential aspects of crisis communication (Griffin, 2012). However, if we accept Grunig's argument that online media has transformed public relations, forcing organisations to think globally about their public relations, then we should revisit cross-cultural communication theory to establish its relevance for crisis communication (Gordon, 2011).

Cross-cultural communication theory

Although cross-cultural communication is generally grouped under communication theory it has been separated here by virtue of its pervasiveness given the current state of communication. In addition, two further criteria can be seen to have impacted the globalisation of organisations and their publics. Sriramesh (2009) argues that the reduction of trade barriers has led to an increase in an organisation's cultural diversity and a greater local recognition of global issues. Therefore, cross-cultural communication is of rising importance for organisations regardless of whether they operate globally or not.

Communicating across cultures became an area of interest after the Second World War when American companies were expanding into Europe and Japan. As Hurn and Tomalin (2013) found the focus was to understand the construction of culture and the link between language and culture in order to reduce the barriers to effective communication. Hurn and Tomalin (2013) view culture as being both invisible and/or implicit and visible and/or explicit. This can be likened to Hall's (1967) iceberg view of culture with only the top of the iceberg being visible above the water line, while the remainder and the majority are hidden below. However, viewing the palpability of culture as a continuum allows for changes in visibility gained as a result of the aforementioned trends in globalisation and its associated expansion, dilution and merging of culture. The cultural iceberg is incessantly melting and reshaping in response to these forces.

Barriers to cross-cultural communication include ethnocentrism, ignorance, fear, laziness and noise, many of which also constitute barriers to other forms of communication (Hurn & Tomalin, 2013). It is notable that noise is of particular importance in the current communication sphere. Trompenaars' (1998 cited in Hurn & Tomalin, 2013) critical enquiry of an individual's relationship with other people, time and nature has also been considered by various scholars. These issues have been dealt with by various cross-cultural theorists. John and Mildred Hall's theory of high- and low-context cultures, Hofstede and Minkov's dimensions of culture and Richard Lewis's three types of culture: linear active, multi active and reactive are associated theories. Slightly different is John Mole's notion of organisational culture stemming from the nature of the organisation, systemic or organic, and the nature of leadership, group or individual (Hurn & Tomalin, 2013).

Milton Bennett's work on sensitivity to culture defines individuals as either ethnocentric, which is characterised by denial, defence and minimisation, or ethnorelativist, which is characterised by acceptance, adoption and integration. His notion of varying sensitivities connects to the concepts of convergence or divergence in communication behaviour (Bennett, 1993 cited in Hurn & Tomalin, 2013). This also connects to the ability to personalise and persuade, with the ethnocentric resistant to challenges and the ethnorelativist more accommodating. However, being an ethnocentric does not preclude elements of ethnorelativitism, and vice versa. Going back to Hall's iceberg analogy, the exposed parts of the iceberg are more susceptible to the aforementioned forces of globalisation.

Giles's (1973 cited in Griffin, 2012) Communication Accommodation Theory links to the concept of ethnorelativism. Giles labels the act of adapting communication to become more similar, as converging communication, in contrast to the process of accentuating difference in communication behaviour, which is labelled as divergent. He further distinguishes divergent communication behaviour into two variants: over-accommodation and maintenance. Over-accommodation is described as patronising or demeaning of the other, while maintenance is viewed as being ignorant or under-accommodating.

What is critical here is the importance of the *others* perception of convergence or divergence. Whilst convergence is regarded as positive and divergence as negative, it is the perception that creates the reality and not necessarily the intent. In addition, converging messages will be regarded positively during a crisis, indicating the importance of correlating the organisational response with the expectations of publics in order to repair a damaged relationship (Giles, 1973 cited in Griffin, 2012). This further highlights the importance of understanding a public's connection to various events or incidents as essential for public relations crisis communication.

Social Identity Theory, while belonging to the remit of communication theory, also has relevance for current cross-cultural communication. Social Identity Theory views group memberships, whether formal or informal, realised or imagined, as affecting our communication (Tajfel, 1979 cited in Griffin, 2012). Jake Harwood's salient claim that "we are not random individuals wandering the planet with no connections to others" further illustrates how an individual's group memberships, whatever form they take, necessarily impact their reactions to communication (Harwood, 1997 cited in Griffin, 2012).

A significant number of organisations, particularly international airlines, operate in a global and diverse cultural arena. It follows that their publics are also going to be globally and culturally diverse (Oliveira, 2013). While this can be an issue in terms of channels of communication it also presents a significant challenge in public relations crisis communications content. These considerations should inform the *how* and *what* of public relations crisis communication. Therefore, a deeper examination of publics within and around a public relations crisis would seem essential in optimising outcomes.

Stakeholder theory

Stakeholder theory was developed in response to the notion of the corporation as a soulless entity, a concept explicated in Bakan's assessment in *The corporation: the pathological pursuit of profit and power* (2004). Balmer et al. (2016) see the birth of this shareholder/stakeholder conundrum coinciding with the birth of the modern corporation and the 1862 British Companies Act which facilitated joint stock companies and the establishment of the shareholder or the stockholder. Many commentators place the naissance of stakeholder theory with Freeman's 1984 work titled *Strategic Management: A Stakeholder Approach* (Stacy, 2013). Freeman expanded on economist Milton Friedman's 1970 assertion that the "There is one and only one social responsibility of business — to use it[s] resources and engage in activities designed to increase its profits so long as it stays within the rules of the game" (Friedman, 2013). However, it is clear that what Friedman points out to be the primary function of business is related to the duty of an organisation to its shareholders, as opposed to its stakeholders.

It is important to understand prevailing concepts related to stakeholders as it impacts an organisation's perspective of their relationships with their publics. Edward Freeman defines a stakeholder as being 'a group or individual who can affect or is affected by the organisation's success' (Freeman, 1984 cited in Stacy, 2013). Stakeholders and publics are similar in constitution but notably the stakeholder, like the shareholder, can affect or be affected by the organisation's failure, particularly within the framework of public relations crisis communication. The salient difference is that the shareholder has a fiduciary relationship while the stakeholder may or may not. However, as observed in the earlier discussion of publics, stakeholder groupings are not fixed or isolated but amorphous and moving.

Since Freeman's work was published there have been a number of developments in stakeholder theory with three prevailing lines of thought: descriptive, instrumental and normative (Zimmer, 2015). Descriptive discourse sees the value of mapping an organisation's stakeholders to facilitate better organisational decision-making through more information gathering. Friedman argues that in descriptive analysis stakeholders are viewed in terms of how the organisation impacts them or how they impact the organisation (Friedman & Miles, 2006). This linear assessment of the relationship is potentially circumspect in the context of the current communication sphere where information exchange is more complex and interrelated.

Zimmer (2015) argues that instrumental discourse builds on the information obtained from descriptive analysis and seeks to identify the connections between stakeholders and the performance of the organisation; it looks at the relationship between the two. Friedman and Miles (2006) see instrumental stakeholders as those the organisation needs to take account of in order to achieve their goals.

Normative discourse concerns the relationship of the stakeholder and organisation and refers to ethics and social responsibility what Zimmer (2015) explains as "what conduct is appropriate for the organisation and what conduct is inappropriate and unacceptable". Friedman and Miles (2006) define normative stakeholders as those possessing legal claims on the organisation.

What is relevant from stakeholder theory for this discussion is whether the primary responsibility of the organisation is solely to the shareholder or to the wider communities of stakeholders which can be termed 'publics'. In addition, Boutilier notes that normative analysis is typically undertaken in response to a crisis that often results in dramatic changes to an organisation (Boutilier, 1994 cited in Zimmer, 2015). The importance that an organisation places on their relationships with publics is a function of whether they view them in descriptive, instrumental or normative terms.

While the relationship between the organisation and its publics as viewed from the organisation's perspective is important, the extension to theory this book proposes concerns the relationship between the organisation and their publics from the public's perspective. During a crisis it is the public's attribution of relationship damage that defines effective organisational crisis communication response. If a public has deemed their relationship with the organisation damaged by an event or incident then the organisation must respond and attempt to repair that relationship before it threatens their relationship with other publics. Snowballing or domino effects can damage interrelationships of publics in the current communication sphere.

Stephens et al. (2005) pose a related question when they assert that currently there is an absence of knowledge surrounding if (or how) organisations adopt or adapt their message strategies to various stakeholder groups during a crisis. While seeking to come to terms with this question by focusing on crises that require complex technical explanations, they touch on a significant element that has been missing from crisis communication theory. This missing element is the role of the publics or stakeholders in determining or defining a relationship as damaged and ascertaining the extent of that damage while distinguishing it from attributions of responsibility. Ultimately the organisation needs to make a judgement on the crisis response strategies, messages and channels of communication. This work seeks to expand on how organisations gather information for these decisions with the aim of improving outcomes in the event of a damaged relationship so that it prevents further deterioration and reduces the potential for contamination of other relationships.

In order to re-focus crisis communication towards publics it is imperative to acknowledge their perception of convergence or divergence, particularly in terms of relationship damage and the related attribution of responsibility. To understand how the above overarching communication theories have impacted crisis communication, primary attention must focus on the development and exploration of specific crisis communication theories. In fact, both Coombs and Heath challenge the proposition that all crisis theories are derivatives of management theories or public relations theories and therefore propose that crisis communication is worthy of its own scholarly discipline (Coombs & Holladay, 2012).

3 Crisis management theory

The development of specific crisis management theories was a process that, according to Coombs (2006), evolved from key tenets of apologia, impression management and image restoration or image repair theory as it is now often referred to. Impression management and image restoration theory can be seen to place the organisation squarely in focus. A delineation of impression and image management is unwarranted given that the focus of this work centres on the public's definition of their relationship to the organisation, and not the other way around.

As explained in the previous chapter, many established communication theories have influenced, or have relevance, to public relations crisis communication. However, it is only recently that specific theories have been generated. Whether this increased theoretical attention can be linked to the changing communication sphere is an interesting question. With the availability (and deregulation) of information, publics are no longer dependent on the organisation as the sole source of information, nor are organisations the sole arbiters of communication. The increasingly amorphous manifestation of the relationship between publics and organisations provides an impetus to find, at the very least, a structural understanding of the relationship, particularly in the fraught circumstances of a public relations crisis.

Apologia

Coombs (2006, p. 176) positions Dionisopolous and Vibbert (1988) as the first theorists to assert that apologia could apply to organisations. Although they did not refer to crisis communication, they argued that organisations are perceived to have a personality by their stakeholders (publics), and therefore they are capable of apologising, should the need arise. This is similar to the earlier assertion that an organisation's image, vision, ethics and behaviour constitute a personality.

This is followed by Ice's (Ice, 1991 cited in Coombs, 2006) examination of Union Carbide's response to the Bhopal Gas tragedy that happened on the night of December 2, 1984. The accident occurred at the Union Carbide pesticide plant in Bhopal, India, and caused the leak of poisonous gases. Over 600,000 people were exposed causing around 15,000 deaths (Taylor, 2014). Ice asserted that Union Carbide's multiple stakeholders ought to be treated separately and can require different responses (Ice, 1991 cited in Coombs, 2006). In 1995, Hobbs explored the notion of combining strategies, thereby reinforcing the notion of tailoring messages or response strategies according to the varying requirements of publics (Hobbs, 1995 cited in Coombs, 2006).

Hearit's (1995) work looks at the organisation's position in terms of its social legitimacy. He looked at the match between an organisation's values and their public's expectations of them, such that an organisation gains social legitimacy by meeting the expectations of their publics. This is in the remit of social judgement theory and supports the significance of the relationship between an organisation and its publics. Hearit argues that a crisis impacts an organisation's social legitimacy and his research identified two strains of response: those where the organisation takes some responsibility for the crisis and those where the organisation denies a crisis exists. Hearit's exposition offers no linkage between what triggers the crisis and the response apart from grouping crisis as stemming from incompetence or irresponsibility. The notion of the public perception of the crisis driving the response is absent, and the onus sits wholly with the organisation. However, he does assert that the organisational response is a public action, which coincides with the earlier assertions that crises occur in the public domain and must be remedied there as well.

The notion of legitimacy is fundamental to both Hearit's work and that of Allen and Caillouet whose 1994 work focused on the link between the crisis response and re-legitimisation, which evolved into impression management. Legitimacy is the belief that stakeholders have in the organisation's intent to follow rules. Any variance is seen as a crisis. The concepts of re-legitimisation and image management link to image restoration theory, which most scholars identify as one of the preeminent works on crisis communication alongside situational crisis communication theory (SCCT) (Botan & Hazleton, 2006).

In this regard Philip and Young (2009, p. 251) comment that "more than ever before it is the actions of an organization that shape reputation, rather than the image crafted for that organization by communications professionals". They also point out that there are multiple publics and channels of communication and all of it cannot be monitored (Philip & Young, 2009, p. 237).

Image restoration theory

William Benoit's theory of Image Restoration, or Image Repair as it is more commonly referred to now, is based on the image or reputation of the organisation. He asserts that an organisation's image or reputation is a very valuable asset, affecting its ability to do business. This image/reputation is subjective and exists in the perceptions of the organisation's publics. An organisation's reputation is damaged when the audiences perceive that it has caused a crisis (Benoit & Pang, 2008). It is imperative to note that image also exists in the organisation's perception of itself.

Benoit's observations are based on two key assumptions. First, that something offensive has occurred, and, second, that the organisation is responsible for the offense. It is the perception of both the offense and responsibility that is critical (Benoit, 1997). This initial link between what Benoit terms 'audience' and perception of responsibility foreshadows the association between 'publics' and responsibility and is significant here as this work proposes a hierarchy of publics related to their attribution of responsibility.

Benoit (1997) identifies the five broad categories of image restoration response as denial, evasion of responsibility, reducing offensiveness of event, corrective action and mortification. However, he refrains from asserting the efficacy of his strategies or providing a causal link between them and the crisis event or the various publics.

Benoit (1997) also makes the important observation that as each audience or public/s has differing responses based on their views it is necessary to prioritise audiences. Though he contends that identifying the relevant audience or public is important to ensure the message is correctly adapted, he does not indicate a rationale or method for doing so. In addition, Benoit does not account for the convergence of publics and media in the current communication sphere. That being said, his theory broke new ground as it has created a typology of organisational response and is arguably the most common starting point in studies of crisis communications.

Situational crisis communication theory (SCCT)

Timothy Coombs built upon Benoit's work by developing SCCT. Coombs positions SCCT as a "theoretical framework to integrate the various ideas that have emerged from the crisis response research" concentrating on the situation as the best indicator of an effective response strategy (Coombs, 2006). His notion of efficacy is important as it would be redundant for an organisation to employ a response that was ineffectual in repairing the relationship between itself and its publics.

Coombs (2006, p. 175) cites Benson's (1998) assertion that specific responses work better in specific situations and asserts that SCCT is the fulfilment of that ideal. To be successful this requires a list of crisis response strategies, a framework for categorising crisis situations and a method for matching the response strategy to the situation. Coombs argued that certain incidents or situations exhibited greater attributions of responsibility, and therefore the response should accept that responsibility. The same holds for moderate attributions and weak attributions of responsibility. Coombs focuses on the event as the indicator of stakeholder attributions of responsibility and compiled the below list of events and corresponding attributions of responsibility:

Strong Attributions of Organisational Crisis Responsibility are:

- Organisational misdeeds
- Management misconduct
- Injuries (external stakeholders deceived and harmed)
- No injuries (external stakeholders deceived but not harmed)
- Human breakdown product recall
- Human breakdown accident

Moderate Attributions of Organisational Crisis Responsibility are:

- Technical breakdown product recall
- Technical breakdown accident
- Mega damage (significant environmental damage)
- Challenge (stakeholders challenging organisation)

Weak Attributions of Organisational Crisis Responsibility are:

- Rumours
- Natural disasters
- Malevolence or product tampering (by external agents)
- Workplace violence (attacks by employees or former employees)
  (Coombs, 2006)

What is also notable from Coombs's SCCT is its use of modifiers in the evaluation of responsibility. He argued that performance history and crisis severity affected the evaluation and notes that initial research indicated that where there is increased severity of personal injuries this equates with increased perceptions of organisational responsibility (Coombs, 2006).

The practicalities of crisis communication are covered by a number of theorists and summarised by Coombs who distinguishes between form and content, where form delineates the activity surrounding crisis communication and content analyses what is being said in the crisis communication (Coombs, 2006). This distinction is useful for crisis communication analysis as it facilitates independent study of methods or channels of communication, the medium as elaborated by McLuhan and the crisis message content.

Coombs (2006, p. 149) identifies three key factors that he describes as essential for successful form, regardless of the medium, which is "be quick, be consistent and be open". These are commonly prescribed for efficiency. For example, Fearn-Banks (2011) refers to the first hour immediately following crisis notification as the "golden hour". This is extremely relevant for the current communication sphere given publics are now communicating with each other independent of the organisation. There have been further reductions to the timing of an organisation's initial crisis communication by various scholars in response to the digitisation of communication.

Coombs' notion of consistency requires that messages from the organisation should be free of contradiction. He cites Clampitt and Garvin who commented that "inconsistency erodes the believability of a message" (Coombs, 2006, p. 173). What is important to note here for international airlines is that this message must remain consistent regardless of geographic location (Coombs, 2006). However, consistency does not necessarily negate tailoring messages or emphasising certain aspects and relegating others according to the attribution of responsibility. This book proposes that tailoring messages facilitates the correlation between the organisation and their publics in terms of their communication response. This creates greater convergence as suggested by Giles's theory and offers the best opportunity for successful crisis communication.

SCCT makes strong inroads towards identifying incidents or situations that have the potential to cause a critical schism in the relationship between an organisation and its publics. Yet it falls short of integrating the convergence of publics in the communication sphere and the function of publics in determining attributions of responsibility. It also overlooks the repercussions this potentially has on the efficacy of crisis communication. In essence, the link between the relevant public and their attributions of responsibility is missing. All publics do not hold equal attributions of responsibility for the same event, instead there exists hierarchy of publics in terms of their attributions of organisational responsibility depending on various factors one of which, as Coombs (2006) correctly identifies, includes the event itself.

However, Coombs and Holladay do acknowledge a shift in research focus from senders of crisis communication to the receivers (the publics) acknowledging that the rationale of crisis communication is based upon the assumption that the messages will affect the crisis publics positively, and this, in turn, will benefit the organisation (Coombs & Holladay, 2014). Given this acknowledgement it is essential to integrate an organisation's publics into crisis communication theory beyond what currently exists.

Excellence theory

Coombs and Holladay's (2014) statement on the receivers of crisis communication leads onto James Grunig's Excellence Theory which explores the communication sphere identifying four typologies of communication: press agentry, public information, two-way asymmetrical and two-way symmetrical; emphasising the last as the preferred and potentially only choice for success given the current media environment (Grunig, 2009).

Grunig (2009) notes that two-way symmetrical communication uses dialogue, amongst other attributes, to manage conflict with both internal and external publics. He acknowledges the convergence of publics within the communication sphere by contending that an organisation simply cannot have and does not need relationships with individuals who are not members of their publics regardless of the fact that they may be communicating with others who are. While it is a logical supposition that two-way symmetrical communication with everyone is not viable for an organisation, it does not mitigate the value of information or one-way symmetrical forms of communications. As Grunig (2009) himself asserts, "digital media now make it easier for publics to form and to establish relationships anywhere in the world". The rationale for ongoing investment in two-way asymmetrical communication is crisis communication. Individuals can instantly become members of an organisation's publics. They can in fact become one of their most important publics, as the result of an event. Making no prior effort to communicate with publics impacts the likelihood of fast and effective crisis communication.

Going back to the concepts of spectators, contributors and originators, it is clear that Grunig's two-way dialogical communication is only relevant for originators and contributors and the spectators are those that Grunig indicates an organisation can ignore. However, this book contends that to make no communicative effort can expose an organisation, particularly in a crisis. This is not to argue that constant two-way dialogical communication can be achieved with every public, but that one-way symmetrical communication with spectators should not be abandoned, as spectators can become contributors and even originators as a result of an event.

But Grunig does not account for hierarchies of crisis publics impacting on the efficacy of crisis communications and instead focuses on what constitutes effective communication, which is two-way symmetrical or dialogical communication (Grunig, 2009). In applying this to crisis communication and differing attributions of organisational responsibility it is paramount for an organisation to employ two-way symmetrical communication with publics who hold high attributions of organisational responsibility and intercessory publics. These publics should be at the top of an organisation's hierarchy of crisis publics.

The rhetorical arena

As mentioned previously, the development of converged and interconnected publics in the current communication sphere is acknowledged by Frandsen and Johansen (2007) in the concept of the Rhetorical Arena. This model of the communication sphere is characterised by a multi-vocal approach, which means it is both sender oriented and receiver oriented such that there is no dominant voice. The rhetorical arena looks at the sphere of crisis communication as a place where many voices interact. Thus, it becomes even more critical for an organisation to employ a hierarchy of crisis publics. This enables the organisation to communicate with the top of the pyramid efficiently, which is with speed and accuracy. As alluded to earlier, two-way symmetrical communication consumes organisational resources, and during a crisis organisational communication comes under increased stress due to the requirements of speed and volume; therefore it is vital to prioritise crisis communication to maximise the efficacy of limited organisational communication resources.

However, the rhetorical arena may also facilitate a solution to tailoring organisational responses according to attributions of responsibility, in that it allows for multiple and simultaneous messages. This is not to argue for an inconsistent organisational response, rather the opportunity that within the organisational response framework certain aspects can be emphasised or relegated according to the concerned public's attribution of responsibility.

Chaos theory

In Priscilla Murphy's work on chaos theory and crisis management she argues that although chaos theory implies a lack of predictability; the opposite is in fact true. Murphy, who was a critic of Jim Grunig's two-way symmetrical model, asserts that chaos theory allows for disorder, diversity, instability and non-linearity, all of which are traits that characterise the communication sphere. In terms of public relations and crisis communication Murphy observes that the public itself is unstable, and it is not just a particular event that causes instability. Interestingly, Murphy highlights speed of action as a principle that is to be applied with chaos theory and unstable publics (Murphy, 1996). If publics cannot be controlled neither can the remedial measures be fool proof.

Social mediated crisis communication model

Recent developments include social mediated crisis communication, put forth by Kristian Hvass when examining the social media activities of Scandinavian Airlines (SAS) during the ash cloud crisis in 2010 (Hvass, 2014). The model is designed to illustrate how the source and form of crisis information impacts the organisation and suggests social mediated crisis response strategies. Most crucial is the observation that multiple publics exist in the sphere of social media. Related to Green's earlier delineation between spectators, originators and contributors, social mediated crisis communication refers to social media creators, social media followers and social media inactives (Liu et al. 2011). The presence of diverse publics with differing responses is ascertained here. In the event of a crisis, messages are received by multiple publics and publics are also connected to each other. There is also transfer of information between traditional and social media (Austin et al. 2012). Hvass (2014) applies SCCT and Social Mediated Crisis Communication to the situation and concludes that, although social media provide a beneficial channel during a crisis without recognising stakeholders' needs, the social media presence alone cannot guarantee success. In effect, Hvass affirms that it is not the nature of the crisis alone that determines if a social media strategy succeeds but what stakeholders need. What is extremely beneficial from his article is the modelling of Social Mediated Crisis Communication, which illustrates how the organisation is excluded from many of the communication flows between the agents of social media.

While this new model is beneficial as it opens up different possibilities for viewing and assessing the communication sphere it only views the relationships in terms of social media, that is social media followers, social media creators and social media inactives sitting alongside traditional media, the organisation and social media. The issue for organisations and their publics is greater and more complex than this model intimates during a public relations crisis.

In order to ascertain the gaps in established theory a case study of Malaysia Airlines MH370 disappearance and post-event communication was conducted. To understand the basics of this analysis the norms of the aviation industry as they apply to crises are delineated in the next chapter.

4   The Malaysia Airlines
       MH370 case

Aviation industry norms

The aviation industry is debatably one of the most precarious in terms
of events or incidents that result in mass injuries or death. As grue-
some as that assertion is, it is also, as frequently touted, one of the
safest modes of transportation.

> Fatal accidents to large passenger aircraft remain rare events. An
> estimated 7% growth in air traffic for 2018 over 2017 puts the rate
> of fatal accidents for large aeroplanes in commercial air transport
> at 0.36 fatal accidents per million flights. That is a rate of one fatal
> accident every 3 million flights. This years' fatal accident rate is
> higher than the most recent 5-year averages (2012–2016: 0.31 and
> 2013–2017: 0.24).
>
> Young, 2019

Jerry Hendin et al. (2008) compare statistics from 2006 where air
crashes resulted in 1,300 deaths globally as opposed to 43,000 deaths
resulting from automobile accidents in America alone. Airline incidents and events are predictable occurrences; however what is not
predictable, and Hendin et al. (2008) concur, is the time and location –
the when and where.

Airlines anticipate incidents; they train their staff repeatedly and
regularly to ensure they are as well prepared as possible, if and when
they occur. In addition, safety regulations are governed and regulated
by a number of independent bodies: namely governments; international bodies, such as the International Air Transport Association
(IATA) and the International Civil Aviation Organisation (ICAO);
and aircraft manufacturers. IATA is the trade body for airlines and
covers 290 airline partners and 82% of the worlds air traffic, providing

the two-letter airline code that precedes flight numbers of member airlines (IATA n.d.).

ICAO is the UN body set up in 1944 after the Convention on Civil Aviation and works closely with IATA to manage international standards and safety, providing the three-letter code that denotes each airline (ICAO n.d.). Given the volume of regulation concerning aviation safety it is plausible to deduce that airlines themselves would be well prepared for any ensuing public relations crisis that follows an event.

However, this is obviously not always the case. Airlines focus heavily on operational response, which is the response to the event as opposed to a response to the public relations issue or crisis that can ensue. There are substantial reports and studies on aviation incidents and events, and IATA uses these reports extensively to improve safety standards. However, they do not engage with the public relations consequences of air incidents or accidents. There are no manuals produced by IATA or ICAO for stakeholder management. In fact, in an amendment to Annex 13 tabled at the second meeting of the Asia Pacific Accident Investigation Group (2014), ICAO introduced the term "contributing factors" in order to focus on the reasons for an event as opposed to the responsibility.

Relating to the above is the belief that aviation events have multiple causes further evidenced by various aviation safety models including the commonly referred to James Reason's Swiss cheese model (Skybrary. aero, 2016). This model, utilised by ICAO in their safety manual, looks to breaches of multiple lines of defence that result in an incident or accident. Interestingly, from the mid-1990s onwards the explanations have extended to include the organisation, factors such as organisational culture, and policies which can now be considered attributing factors (ICAO Safety Management Manual, 3rd edition, 2013).

If publics relations crisis is viewed as an issue that occurs between an organisation and one or more of its publics then it follows that the organisation is primarily responsible for the crisis communications that have the potential to resolve the crisis. This is not to say that the organisation in question cannot be a peak body. It must be noted that IATA and ICAO would definitely be considered publics of an airline.

Aviation crises

An aviation public relations crisis is one that results from an event which causes an immediate schism in the relationship with the organisation's publics such that it threatens other relationships and the viability of the organisation. It could also be a public relations issue that is not managed appropriately and emerges into a crisis. That is, the initial relationship damage is minor but due to the mis-management of the issue it develops into a crisis.

It is still important to emphasise the difference between a public relations issue and a public relations crisis. Some commentators have branded airline issues as crises. For example, the case of United Airlines in which a disgruntled passenger posted a song on YouTube about United Airlines damaging his guitar and refusing to pay the repair bill which went viral. However, given the earlier definition this paper argues that this is an example of an incident becoming an issue but not a crisis (Pang et al. 2013). Kevin Smith's experience cited in the same article is similar. Kevin Smith was ejected from an aircraft by Southwest Airlines for being "too fat to fly", too large to occupy one seat. Smith took to social media, ranting against Southwest and gaining attention for the issue of overweight passengers. Again, this should be viewed as an issue and not a crisis. The rationale is that the relationship schism is not acute in terms of its effects on the organisation.

Empirical study

The disappearance of Malaysia Airlines MH370 is an example of a crisis resulting from an event and is a worthy starting point for the development of an extension to existing theory.

The best test of theory is to apply it to a real-life situation. Therefore, to assess the proposed revision to the hierarchy of publics theory a live case study of the crisis communication that followed the disappearance of Malaysia Airlines MH370 has been chosen. Eisenhardt's (1989) work 'Building Theories from Case Study Research' and Robert K. Yin's (2003, p. 1) treatise on *Case study Research Designs and Methods* confirms that "case studies are the preferred strategy when 'how' or 'why' questions are being posed, when the investigator has little control over events, and when the focus is on a contemporary phenomenon within some real-life context". The contemporary phenomenon studied here in the real-life context is the response of organisations to publics during airline disasters.

The situation of MH370 is unique in that the circumstances of the aircraft's disappearance remain unknown. However, the context of the airline's communication with key publics during and post crisis is universal. The use of an instrumental case study helps to move beyond the specific situation studied. Stake (1995, p. 137) comments that an instrumental case "provides insight into an issue or helps to refine a theory. The case is of secondary interest; it plays a supportive role, facilitating our understanding of something else". An in-depth analysis of the case helps the researcher to find what he pursues beyond the case. Stake (1995, p. 137) clarifies that the instrumental case does not have to be typical of other cases.

Researchers use multiple data collection methods like interviews, observations, archival sources, physical artefacts, newspaper clippings and other articles appearing in the mass media or in community newsletters (Eisenhardt, 1989, p. 537; Yin, 2004, pp. 83–86). Online press statements were the primary data sources evaluated in this study.

While there were a number of social media channels, including more than 60 Twitter accounts featuring MH370 in their handle and more than 700 groups on Facebook featuring MH370 (or a derivative) in their title, analysis was not performed on these resources. Repeated attempts to get permission to access the social media platforms were unsuccessful. Nonetheless, the volume of data on the social media platforms is an indication of the variety and vastness of information publics are exposed to. To minimise data saturation a date range was set for the online press releases analysed. However, a selection of subsequent releases were analysed to ensure no unique communication threads were ignored.

One of the authors played the role of a participant observer because of extensive experience with and knowledge of the aviation industry. This allowed for candid observation and triangulation of data and ensuing construct validity as Yin (2004, p. 99) recommends. Authors functioning as participant observers is common in case studies. For example, the lead author in 'The use of Case study Method in Theory testing: The example of Steel eMarketplaces' (Iacono et al. 2011) was also a participant observer.

All data units were coded before qualitative analysis as factual, empathetic or defensive or a combination of these. Some press releases have more than one code as their content mirrors multiple dimensions. A qualitative thematic content analysis of the press statements was done using Nvivo to identify predominant themes. In addition, the releases were assessed against both Benoit's image restoration strategies and Coombs's situational crisis communication theory (SCCT). This was done to accurately correlate organisational acceptance of responsibility against the public's attributions of responsibility.

Extant data and contextual positioning

Charmaz (2006, p. 37) refers to data collected and not generated as 'extant' data. This study uses extant data as it relies on press releases.

The researcher needs to establish the context of their interaction with the extant data in order to form the basis of the analysis (Ralph et al. 2014). The authors develop a detailed list of sample questions to help establish the 'contextual positioning'.

The questions in Table A4.1 have been chosen from those suggested by Ralph et al. (2014, p. 5) and help to define the context.

MH370 case: summary

The study of Malaysia Airlines MH370 is of particular interest given the obvious failure of the organisation in their crisis communication. The dissension and hostility of the families of the passengers and the increasing volume of communications from the Malaysian Government are indicators of a failure in crisis communication. Furthermore, the causes of disappearance of MH370 remain a mystery adding to the enigma. Discussing the many theories and conjectures that have ensued, though interesting, is beyond the scope of this book, and hence such a discussion is not included.

MH370 was a Malaysia Airlines flight that departed Kuala Lumpur in the early hours of Saturday, March 8, 2014 but never arrived at its Beijing destination. It had 239 passengers and crew on board, and the announcement that the plane had gone missing was made by Malaysia Airlines CEO, Ahmad Jauhari Yahya, an hour after its expected arrival.

Malaysia Airlines was formed in 1937 and became the national airline of Malaysia in 1947. After Singapore separated from Malaysia the airline became a bi-national carrier until the partnership was dissolved in 1972 and the airline was renamed as Malaysia Airlines System Berhad (MAS) and returned to being Malaysia's national carrier. In July 2015 a new airline Malaysia Airlines Berhad replaced MAS following a Ministry of Finance bill tabled in November 2014 that provided for the establishment of the new carrier (Subramaniam, 2014). A new CEO, Christoph Mueller, an aviation expert of international repute, was appointed after the group chief executive officer stepped down at the end of May 2015 (ch-aviation, 2015).

It is important to acknowledge that Malaysia Airlines was not in the best financial shape when MH370 disappeared. The company had generated chequered financial results during the preceding eight years (Thomas, 2015). However, when comparing the losses for a nine-month period in 2013 with the same period in 2014 the figures are vastly different. The 2013 loss totalled Malaysian Ringgit 827 million compared with approximately Malaysian Ringgit 1.3 billion in 2014 (Topham,

2015). It is also significant that there was a second incident in July of the same year (2014) when MH17 was shot down over Eastern Ukraine. While the MH17 incident is not the focus of this illustrative study it must be considered a factor in the demise of the airline.

The press releases on the Malaysia Airlines website for the MH17 incident reveal that media statements from the airline are not attributed to any specific member of staff but are generic and relatively few in number (only 15). In comparison, the response to the MH370 incident was prolific with 28 releases in the first 30 days post the disappearance and 45 releases in total over 2 years. The only statements on MH17 credited to specific people are those made by Najib Razak, the Malaysian Prime Minister; YB Dato' Sri Liow Tiong Lai, the Malaysian Minister of Transport; and Datuk Dr Wee Ka Siong, Minister in the Malaysian Prime Minister's Department (Malaysian Airlines MH17, 2019).

Examining the communications generated by the Malaysian Government in response to the MH370 and MH17 events is important. First, international aviation events assume the dimension of international political events as they usually involve numerous governments, either because of the nationality of the passengers and crew or because of the location of the event. Second, international airlines represent the country where they are based regardless of whether they are state-owned or private enterprises. Lastly and most importantly, in the MH370 incident, the Government is also a public in the crisis communication.

Analysis of relevant press releases

The official press statements analysed in this study were posted on the Malaysia Airlines dark site and are now visible via the Press Room link on the home page of Malaysia Airlines' main website.

Table A4.2 details the press statements made by Malaysia Airlines from March 8, 2014, the day of the event, to April 8, 2014, one month post the event. Some of the 'Wh' questions raised by Ralph et al. (2014, p. 5) for contextual positioning are responded to in the table. A summary of the press releases and the byline is also included. While all the statements are labelled media statements, it is clear from the content that some of the releases are directed to other stakeholders too. The audience of the statements have been identified as Media, Family and General. 'Media' refers to local and international media organisations and representatives, 'Family' signifies the next of kin of the passengers and crew of MH370 and 'General' stands for the greater community of publics (both local and international) who are exposed

Figure 4.1 Qualitative analysis of Malaysia airlines' statements (entire period) word frequency generated by Nvivo.

Figure 4.2 Qualitative analysis of Malaysian government's statements (entire period) word frequency provided by nvivo.

to communications regarding the disappearance of MH370 without being directly connected to the event.

Table A4.3 details statements made by Malaysia Airlines after the one month initial period; these are coded the same as Table A4.2.

Table A4.4 details statements made by the Malaysian Government Representatives, featured on the Malaysia Airlines website as official communication. Here again the same coding scheme was applied.

In addition to the above, qualitative assessments were performed on the media statements from both Malaysia Airlines and the Malaysian Government to establish word counts and most frequently utilised terms across both sets of statements. These are represented in infographs as generated by Nvivo in Figures 4.1 and 4.2.

Observations and discussion

On assessing the 29 Malaysia Airlines statements made in the first 31 days post the disappearance of MH370 it was observed that the content of most messages was factual, followed by defensive messages; empathetic messages were fewest in number. All releases, except one, were in both English and Mandarin. The content of these releases were overwhelmingly factual yet they were also significantly defensive and were in response to media stories and reactions of families.

During the first three days, the statements were factual and empathetic. However, from day four onwards they became increasingly defensive in response to various media reports including rumours of passengers who failed to board, allegations against the first officer, speculation on the culpability of the pilots, as well as issues with Chinese next of kin and questions about the transparency of Malaysia Airlines communication.

The nationalities of the passengers were issued three times, with various corrections, and it took over 24 hours before a dedicated family line was set up in either Malaysia or China. In contrast during the MH17 incident there was a dedicated family line within nine hours of the last known contact with the aircraft and within seven hours of the announcement of the event. The dedicated family contact line was not made available until the early hours of Sunday morning, announced in the sixth statement. Until then there were only two lines – a general public line and a media one. In addition, it was six days before flight numbers connected to MH370 were retired but with MH17 it took only three days.

There were only two statements attributed to the Chairman and Group Chief Executive Officer of Malaysia Airlines, Ahmad Jauhari

Yahya, during this period. Although he was present at the televised press conferences, he did not lead them. The involvement of senior management in crisis communication conveys the message that the organisation views the crisis as serious, so serious that it warrants the attention of the Chief Executive Officer and senior management representatives. Therefore the absence of statements attributed to Malaysia Airlines senior management can be seen to have been detrimental to Malaysia Airlines' crisis communication efforts.

According to the data analysed the first statement that was attributed directly to Ahmad Jauhari Yahya was on March 25, 2014, over two weeks from the MH370 event and the day after the Prime Minister's announcement that MH370 had been deemed to have ended in the Indian Ocean with no survivors. This statement coincided with the release of an interview of the Chairman and Group CEO by the BBC's Alastair Leithead (2014) where he defended the actions of Malaysia Airlines against accusations by the interviewer that the company has not done enough for the families.

Malaysia Airlines was also criticised for the use of short messaging service (SMS) to notify some of the relatives about the incident preceding the aforementioned announcement by the Malaysian Prime Minister. They repeated the same error less than a year later when the official declaration that MH370 was judged an accident according to the Chicago convention was announced. Malaysia Airlines defended its use in the first instance arguing that they only had 30 minutes to notify over 1,000 people, and they wanted the families to hear it first from the airline. This defence did not achieve traction with the next of kin.

The timing of the statement suggests lack of coordination between Malaysia Airlines and the Malaysian Government. The Malaysian Prime Minister made the televised announcement just before 22:00 hours (Malaysian time) after a briefing by representatives from the United Kingdom's Air Accident Investigation Branch. Malaysia Airlines argued there was insufficient time for them to speak to all of the next of kin and defended the use of SMS. Further, the absence of a Malaysia Airlines representative at the press conference added to the imbroglio.

The top three terms appearing in the Malaysia Airlines releases are 'airlines' (appearing 228 times), 'Malaysia' (appearing 223 times) and 'families' (appearing 199 times). 'Passengers', 'support' and 'media' as key words appear 87, 81 and 76 times, respectively. From this it is clear that Malaysia Airlines identified families as their most important public. However, the response strategy the airline employed when dealing with the families was not successful as evidenced from various statements. Of particular note is statement #30 concerning the restraining of Malaysia Airlines staff by families in Beijing. By analysing the response strategies employed by the airline against prevailing public relations crisis theory we can identify how they failed but not necessarily why.

While assessing the first 30 days' releases in terms of Benoit's image restoration strategies two significant strategies were identified. Malaysia Airlines emphasised details of compensation given and constantly publicised efforts taken to assist the families. These would help the airline to appear to be fulfilling their responsibility and also mitigate criticism. The airline repeatedly highlighted that the tragedy had affected them as much as the families using statements like "... Malaysia Airlines are similarly anxious" in releases #9 and #10, and "It must be remembered too that 13 of our own colleagues and fellow Malaysians were also on board" in release #27. In their attempt to avoid hurting sentiments and evade responsibility, Malaysia Airlines' crisis communication with the families of those on board and the media was ineffective. The reason for this lies in incongruence between the attribution of responsibility held by the families and the acceptance of responsibility by Malaysia Airlines. It is therefore clear that Malaysia Airlines did not accurately assess the attributions of responsibility of their priority publics.

When applying Coombs's SCCT the strategy that Malaysia Airlines employed can be seen as indicative of ingratiation, emphasising the good deeds they were doing for the families. The airline also employed the excuse strategy by arguing that they had no control over the event, both of which are deemed to have a mild acceptance of responsibility. According to Coombs's theory, where there is a high attribution of responsibility the better strategy is one that has a very high acceptance of responsibility (Coombs, 2006).

However, Coombs does not look at where a public is positioned in relation to the event or subsequent crisis but focuses on the event itself. This is not to say that Coombs should be disregarded; in fact, both Benoit and Coombs should be referred to. The issue is they do not include the complete scenario when assessing attributions of responsibility and therefore do not provide the most effective indicator of organisational response.

When correlating the response to the event it becomes problematic, particularly for international airlines, although this is not exclusively so. Coombs (2006) argues that where an organisation is deemed to purposefully place stakeholders at risk, those stakeholders shall hold high attributions of organisational responsibility. Therefore, the organisation should utilise either full apology or corrective action, both of which, according to Coombs, correlate to a high acceptance of responsibility.

Herein lies the challenge raised by SCCT for Malaysia Airlines' crisis communications after the MH370 incident. The airline did not purposefully place stakeholders at risk; therefore it can be argued that Malaysia Airlines were correct in their communication response strategy, which was to minimise their responsibility. In addition, as the circumstances of the event remain unknown to a large extent all aspects of Coombs theory cannot be applied. For instance, the cause of the event has not yet been determined as human error, technical failure or other certain causes, and this makes it difficult to accurately assess the 'situation'. In addition, while Coombs's *severe personal injury modifier* applies in this instance it is not an event or situation descriptor, and therefore the aforesaid issue remains. Further, Coombs's attributions of responsibility are defined by the event itself. However, it is not a certainty that organisations and their publics will hold the same evaluation of an event, as can be seen in the case of MH370. Also, regardless of the situation, publics can still hold high attributions of responsibility by virtue of their proximity to the event as opposed to the event itself.

Considering both Coombs and Benoit's principles it is clear that Malaysia Airlines' crisis communication strategies were mismatched with the attributions of responsibility of the next of kin. While the event is a significant indicator of attributions of responsibility, it is not the only consideration that an organisation needs to make. The organisation also needs to consider the public's attribution of responsibility, influenced not only by the typology of the event but also by their proximity to the event.

The public that is most affected by the event, that is closest to the event, whose relationship with the organisation has been severed, will hold the highest attribution of responsibility. It is not enough to nominate key publics in a crisis; organisations also need to assess their varying attributions of responsibility and respond accordingly. Interestingly it is Coombs who mentions Ice's Union Carbide study, which notes varying responses to the Bhopal event to mend relationship with stakeholder (Coombs, 2006). Notably, it has already been attested by Ice that different publics require different responses because, as this book suggests, they have different attributions of organisational responsibility.

Let us consider another of Malaysia Airlines' publics: the Malaysian Government. During the 31-day period from March 8, 2014–April 8, 2014, there were 17 statements made by the Malaysian Government as opposed to Malaysia Airlines' 29 statements. Interestingly, from day 1 to day 12 only 12% of statements were attributed to Malaysian Government representatives, whereas from day 13 to day 31 the figure rises to 70%. It is clear from these figures that the Malaysian Government became more heavily involved in the crisis communication.

One potential reason is their dissatisfaction with the crisis communication of Malaysia Airlines therefore intimating a schism in the airlines' relationship with another of its publics. Other reasons include the international and political involvement that made this a diplomatic issue with deployment of international search teams and a significant number of Chinese families expressing stern dissatisfaction with Malaysia Airlines.

The Malaysian Government's statements were overwhelmingly factual during the first 31 days and beyond, and due to the lack of translation into Mandarin, it can be argued that they were directed not to the next of kin but predominantly to the media. There were only five bi-lingual releases during the first 31 days, and from April 8, 2014, onwards releases were exclusively in English.

Coombs's rules of form: be quick, consistent and open

According to Coombs (2007, p. 128) the rules of form are to be quick, consistent and open. He does distinguish openness in two ways – referring to either availability of the organisation to stakeholders or full disclosure. Given the legal framework that most organisations operate under, full disclosure is not viable; however, availability most certainly is. Malaysia Airlines was slow to respond, particularly with respect to the families based in China. The dedicated family line took time to set up, and the airline was slow to retire the flight numbers. They were inconsistent in their statements, particularly in the first few days, with multiple errors in the passenger list. Most critically, Malaysia Airlines was not open. Senior management was not available as evidenced by the lack of statements attributed to a representative of the airline, senior or not. It is clear that the *form* of Malaysia Airlines' crisis communications was not effective.

Content strategies

Malaysia Airlines adhered to two of Benoit's (1997) strategies of response: bolstering and compensation, both of which, according to Benoit, reduce the offensiveness of the event. In addition, given that the event cannot be clearly defined due to lack of evidence Malaysia Airlines was justified in pursuing Coombs's strategies of ingratiation and excuse, both of which are deemed to have a mild acceptance of responsibility. Although Benoit's strategies are descriptive not prescriptive, Coombs's SCCT is designed to be the latter. The difficulty arises when the event cannot be clearly defined. What is clear, however, is that the content strategies employed by Malaysia Airlines were unsuccessful. The evidence of this lies in the actions of a number of publics, namely the Chinese next of kin, the Malaysian Government and subsequently the families of Malaysia Airlines crew.

Relationship with publics

From the statements we can deduce that there was hostility between the Chinese next of kin and Malaysia Airlines. There are a number of references to meetings between the Airline's representatives and the families in Beijing not going well, the restraining of Malaysia Airlines staff and the assaulting of a member of staff in Beijing. There was also the defence of Malaysia Airlines' use of SMS to give information to the families from which we can deduce this action was not well received. In addition, the Malaysian Government took over the crisis communication from the airline after about two weeks post the event. The absence of the Airline's representatives at the most significant press conference announcing that the plane may have ended its flight in the Indian Ocean also indicates that the relationship between Malaysia Airlines and the Malaysian Government was strained. Further, the dissolving of the airline by the Government and subsequent institution of a 'new' airline attests to the degree of damage in the relationship between the organisation and one of its publics.

It is clear that Malaysia Airlines acknowledged the families of the passengers as one of their most important publics but their communication with them was ineffective. This necessitates creating a hierarchy of publics that accounts for varying attributions of responsibility. It would close the gap between the expectations of the publics and the responses of the organisation. By employing a hierarchy of crisis publics the organisation is able to clearly tailor its communication strategies to achieve congruence between the expectations of their publics and their crisis communication response. It is not enough to nominate key publics in a crisis. An understanding of each public's expectations is required in order to effectively communicate through the crisis. Further, by meeting these expectations the domino effect on other relationships within the communication sphere is mitigated.

The case of MH370 reveals a missing element in current crisis communication theory. It has been alluded to and is supported by existing theory but has yet to be fully explored as an important facet of public relations crisis communication.

Appendix

Table A4.1 Contextual Positioning of Extant Data

Questions	Responses
Who conceived, supported, shaped, wrote, edited and published the text?	*Malaysia Airlines and/or a sanctioned authority*
Who was its production intended to benefit?	*Various Publics, including but not limited to Media and Families of those on board*
What stated or assumed purpose does it serve?	*Data serves as an officially sanctioned information portal*
What specific value does this text bring to the current study?	*It provides an opportunity to assess the efficacy of the above in the context of current crisis communication recommendations and the proposed model of a hierarchy of publics*
What are the parameters of information?	*Two-way asymmetrical communication in response to ongoing events related to the disappearance of MH370*
When was the document conceived, produced and updated?	*Each release was conceived and produced immediately before release, there are no lengthy timelines or observable guidelines for the documents' production*
What is the document's intended lifespan?	*Each release is live until a subsequent release, however they are observable in perpetuity altering the actual lifespan*
To what extent are the issues that influenced and informed the production of this document relevant to the temporal context of the current study?	*They are relevant as they constitute the organisation's immediate official crisis communication response*
Where was the document produced?	*Malaysia Airlines*
Where is the document intended for use?	*As an online resource or information portal*
Why would the text be used?	*To gain information about the disappearance of MH370 and also to gain insight into the relationship between the organisation and its publics*
Why, if at all, is the text unique, reliable and consistent?	*The text is reliable as it is officially sanctioned by the organisation*
How is the text written?	*There are a number of formats utilised and the tone of the message varies*
How is the document achieving its purpose?	*This is the question we are seeking to answer – whether the document does achieve its purpose?*

Table A4.2 Malaysia Airlines Media Statements March 8, 2014–April 8, 2014 (Malaysia Airlines MH370, 2019)

Date	Statement Number and source	When to say it? * (GMT +8)	What to say? (Summary of content)	How to say it?	Who to say it to?
DAY 1					
Sat Mar 8, 2014	1	07:30	Brief announcement of missing air craft / contact # for families	Factual	General
Sat Mar 8, 2014	2	09:05	Statement of regret / More information on flight / Next of Kin support centre in Kuala Lumpur / Phone number for Public / Different phone number for media	Factual / Empathetic	Families and Media
Sat Mar 8, 2014	3	10:30	Flight information / Unconfirmed landing at Nanming / Details of passenger nationalities and pilots / Working with search and rescue team to locate the aircraft	Factual	General
Sat Mar 8, 2014	4 Flight Incident Update	14:30	Reiterating previous information / No information on location of aircraft / Sending a team to Beijing	Factual	Incident Update
Sat Mar 8, 2014	5	16:20	No information on aircraft location / Passenger manifest held until all families contacted / "Go Team" deployed to Beijing / Correction of Nationalities information due to confusion between Indonesia and India country code / Acknowledges unofficial reports in the media	Factual	Media
Sat Mar 8, 2014	6	19:20	International search and rescue mission mobilised / Passenger manifest released and nationality list updated	Factual	Media

(Continued)

Table A4.2 Continued

Date	Statement Number and source	When to say it? *(GMT +8)*	What to say? (Summary of content)	How to say it?	Who to say it to?
DAY 2					
Sun Mar 9, 2014	7	02:00	24 hour mark / Dispatching information as and when MAS receive it / Monitor situation in Beijing / Sole priority to provide assistance to families of passengers / New phone numbers for families in both Kuala Lumpur and Beijing	Factual	Media
Sun Mar 9, 2014	8	09:30	First mention of financial aid to families / Another team of caregivers en route Beijing / Confirmed meeting of MAS senior officials with media and families / Closing comment is reassuring the transparency of MAS communications	Factual	Media
Sun Mar 9, 2014	9	02:43	First statement by Malaysian Airlines Group CEO: Ahmad Yayha	Empathetic	Families Solely
DAY 3					
Mon Mar 10, 2014	10	10:00	Introduction of Department of Civil Aviation (DCA) and more details of efforts for families – reiteration of transparency of Malaysian Airlines and positioning of company as similarly distressed and in need of support	Empathetic / Defensive	Families / Media
Mon Mar 10, 2014	11	17:30	Emergency Operations Centre / Family Management / Search & Rescue / Common Media Enquiries	Factual / Defensive	Media / General
DAY 4					
Tues Mar 11, 2014	12	11:15	Search and Rescue update / Details on actual aircraft / Family task force / Reiterates that MAS will continue to be transparent	Factual	General / Media
Tues Mar 11, 2014	13	17:29	Responding to claims about five failed to board passengers	Factual / Defensive	Media / General
Tues Mar 11, 2014	14	23:30	Response to allegations about first officer	Factual / Defensive	Media / General

	Date	Time	Content	Tone	Audience
DAY 5					
	Wed Mar 12, 2014	01:00	Family assistance – financial and other aid / Support / 115 Family members in Kuala Lumpur supported by 72 caregivers	Factual / Defensive	Media / General
	Wed Mar 12, 2014	11:30	Family Assistance – addressing families in Beijing – 112 caregivers deployed / 94 caregivers (including senior management of MAH) deployed straightaway to Beijing / Use of translators and continuing press conferences with Chinese media / Involvement of DCA / Reiterating passenger families as top priority and transparency of communication	Factual / Defensive	Media / General
DAY 6					
	Thurs Mar 13, 2014	00:45	Refutes claims that some families were flown to India instead of Malaysia	Defensive	Media / General
	Thurs Mar 13, 2014	11:10	Retiring of the flight numbers MH 370 / 371 as a sign of respect	Factual	Families / Media / General
DAY 7					
	Fri Mar 14, 2014	12:13	Reiterating full support of DCA/ Ministry of Transport / Aware of ongoing media speculation but have nothing to add to information already released / Reiterate support to families and regular updates on all matters affecting MH370	Defensive	Media / General
DAY 8					
	Sat Mar 15, 2014	17:45	Follow up of Malaysian PM press-con / Defends keeping information until it has been analysed and verified despite ongoing media speculation / Insinuating that this speculation has added to anguish of families / Reiterates sharing information in a transparent manner – but making sure the information is validated	Factual / Defensive	General / Media

(Continued)

Table A4.2 Continued

Date	Statement Number and source	When to say it? * (GMT +8)	What to say? (Summary of content)	How to say it?	Who to say it to?
DAY 9					
Sun Mar 16, 2014	21	05:15	Revising enquiry phone numbers to a dedicated family line and then another two numbers for media enquiries	Factual / Empathetic (last sentence)	General / Media
DAY 11					
Tues Mar 18, 2014	22 General Press Statement (Joint with Govt.)	17:30	Search Update / ACARS clarification – ACARS disabled and then aircrafts transponder switched off	Factual	General / Media
DAY 12					
Wed Mar 19, 2014	23	16:10	Family response – move to an enhanced Family Support Centre based in KL / SMS blasts and dedicated email for families / Toll free numbers set up in eight countries / Comment on order of communication has always been families first, then media, then public when new information received / Conflicting info and 'wild speculation' has caused distress to families / Again top priority is families of passengers	Factual / Defensive	Media / General
DAY 15					
Sat Mar 22, 2014	24	10:45	Clarification about lithium ion batteries on board – their carriage complied with IATA and ICAO regulations	Factual	Media
Mon Mar 24, 2014	25	10:15	Note that this has already been shared with family members – have to assume that MH370 has ended in Southern Indian Ocean	Empathetic	Media / General

DAY 18

			Time			
Tues Mar 25, 2014	26		00:30	Acknowledged that MAS contacted the majority of families in advance by phone or in person ahead of the Prime Minister's press conference / SMS only used as additional means	Factual	Families / Media / General
Tues Mar 25, 2014	27	Chairman and Group CEO of MAS	12:30	Acknowledgement of Prime Minister's message that aircraft is lost and there were no survivors / CEO adds more details – sorrow for families' loss, comment that MAS also lost colleagues and Malaysians / Clarification that the SMS communication was only as an additional means of communication of the news so the nearly 1,000 family members received the news from MAS and not the media / reiteration of the support provided to date by MAS' 700 caregivers – 2 per family / Accommodation, travel, meals and other expenses, USD 5,000 per passenger to next of kin / Close with description as unprecedented event	Factual / Empathetic / Defensive	Families / Media / General

DAY 21

Fri Mar 28, 2014	28	Chairman and Group CEO of MAS	10:15	Again difficulty of breaking the news of the loss of MH370 to families in short time before Prime Minister's public announcement / thankful for support of International and Malaysian Governments / Malaysia Airlines will take families to Perth should physical wreckage be found / Comments on harm that speculation causes families / Thanking media outlets that have been responsible in reporting MH370 / Release of information under strict control / families priority	Factual / Empathetic / Defensive (English Only)	Families / Media / General

DAY 23

Sun Mar 30, 2014	29	Chairman and Group CEO of MAS	15:45	MAS clarification that it will only send families to site once wreckage found / Continued cooperation with authorities and support for families	Factual / Defensive	Families / Media / General

* Both Kuala Lumpur and Beijing are GMT +8.

Table A4.3 Malaysia Airlines Media Statements March 8, 2014–April 8, 2016. (Malaysia Airlines MH370, 2019)

Date	Statement Number and source	When to say it?* (GMT +8)	What to say?	How to say it?	Who to say it to?
DAY 49					
Fri Apr 25, 2014	30	19:40	Reporting of incident at Lido Hotel in Beijing where members of Malaysia Airlines staff were held from 3pm on the 24th until 1:44am on the 25th by Chinese families "expressing their dissatisfaction" – Upset at not having a Malaysian official at the meeting. Another incident on 22nd where Malaysian Airlines security supervisor was kicked by "aggressive" family member who demanded access to the secretariat – Malaysia Airlines has filed a police report	Factual (English Only)	Media / General
DAY 55					
Thurs May 01, 2014	31 Chairman and Group CEO of MAS	19:00	Detailed release / Despite best efforts (probably the largest search in history) the fate of missing passengers remains unknown / Acutely conscious of families' feelings – they feel the same and are doing whatever they can / Families in hotels no longer will receive updates in the "comfort of their own homes" closing all family assistance centres by May 7 / Detailed plan for follow-up will be sent in person to the families / Reference to financial compensation for 'entitled' Next of kin / Home airline to contact families to initiate advanced compensation payment process / List of documents that were released to families and public on May 1	Factual / (English Only)	Media / General / Families

DAY 56

Fri May 02, 2014	32 Media Statement	21:30	Clarification of issues some related to documents released yesterday – Malaysians on board / Exchange of signals and Cargo carried	Factual (English Only)	Media / General

DAY 57

Sat May 03 2014	33 Media Statement	11:00	Confirms representatives from Family Support Centres have been in touch with Next of Kin to initiate advance compensation payment process / Compensation matters to remain private 'out of respect to grieving families'	Factual / Defensive (English Only)	Media / General

Day 73

Mon May 19, 2014	34 Media Statement	18:45	Defence of media claims that MAS has abandoned families of MH370 crew who are seeking legal help. Some MAS crew have contracted foreign lawyers to represent them so MAS is speaking to their legal reps but speaking directly to those without legal counsel	Factual / Defensive (English Only)	Media / General

DAY 77

Fri May 23, 2014	35 Media Statement	19:45	MAS reiterates its commitment to family members of MH370 / After closure of family assistance centres MAS staff remain in contact and still have the Family Support Centre functioning / Discussion of legal protocols now that some crew member families have legal representation	Factual (English Only)	Media / General

DAY 100

Sun Jun 15, 2014	36 Chairman and Group CEO of MAS	13:00	100 days post-MH370 disappearance / Thoughts with the families of those on board MH370 – we feel their anguish and like them seek answers to find out what happened to MH370 / Thank Governments and agencies from Malaysia, Australia and China plus general reference to others / MAS continues to support search and next of kin and continues to keep in touch / Longest and most painful 100 days in MAS history	Empathetic (English Only)	Media / General / Families

(Continued)

Table A4.3 Continued

Date	Statement Number and source	When to say it? * (GMT +8)	What to say?	How to say it?	Who to say it to?
DAY 248					
Mon Nov 10, 2014	38 Media Statement by MAS	19:30	Response to news articles speculating about official declaration of loss of MH370 / MAS guided by technical team and recovery operations will continue / Airline shares the pain and anguish of family members and are as determined as the families to find answers / Compensation – fair and reasonable in accordance with the law / Family members remain main priority	Factual / Defensive (English Only)	Media / General / Families
DAY 328					
Thurs Jan 29, 2015	39 Media Statement by MAS	20:05	More than 10 months after flight went missing / Declaration of MH370 as an accident official declaration that all lives on board lost / Fair and reasonable compensation in accordance with applicable laws will be made / More resources to Family Support Centre in KL and Family Communications and Support Centre in Beijing – additional Mandarin speakers / MAS HR main contact for families of crew members	Factual (English Only) (Links to both Mandarin and English versions of official declaration by Director General of Civil Aviation Malaysia)	Media / General / Families

DAY 331					
Sun Feb 01, 2015	40 Media Statement by MAS	16:35	MAS clarifies manner in which Next of Kin were informed of Declaration of Accident to flight MH370, Next of Kin in China were notified via text messages by staff at Beijing centre / Next of Kin in Malaysia and around the world were called and only if calls unanswered were notified by text message	Factual / Defensive (English Only)	Media / General
DAY 342					
Thurs Feb 12, 2015	41 Media Statement by MAS	16:35	MAS Group CEO met with 3 of the 15 Chinese next of kin who arrived at MAS headquarters today / MAS in no position to provide clarification or technical information other than what has already been released / MAS information on the investigation will be shared when it is available	Defensive (English only)	Media / General (In response to incident at MAS HQ)
1 Year					
Mon Mar 09, 2015	42 Media Statement by MAS	13:30	Release of Interim Statement of Safety Investigation / MAS "lost 13 dear friends and colleagues" we also want to find out the answers / MAS cooperated fully with investigation / Complies with two points in interim report / MAS clarifies IATA and IOSA plus flight tracking and monitoring systems being enhanced / New system provides actual as well as projected aircraft track	Factual / Defensive (English Only)	Media / General

(Continued)

Table A4.3 Continued

Date	Statement Number and source	When to say it? * (GMT +8)	What to say?	How to say it?	Who to say it to?
13+ Months					
Tues Apr 28, 2015	43 Media Statement by MAS	17:30	Closure of Beijing Communication and Support Centre +6 regional offices / Reconfirm its commitment / Will use several platforms to communicate including dedicated email and phone lines for compensation / New official website www.mh370.gov.my / MAS will continue to explore available avenues to reach out to the families	Factual (English Only)	Media / Families / General
14+ Months					
Fri May 22, 2015	44 Media Statement by MAS	12:45	Response to reports of staged protest at closure of Chinese support facilities / Will not be reopening the centres / Held a face-to-face engagement on May 15 in Beijing	Factual (English Only)	Media / Families / General
16+ Months					
Thurs Jul 30, 2015	45 Media Statement by MAS	08:45	Discovery of flaperon at Reunion Island / Too early to comment	Factual (English Only)	Media / General

	No.		Time	Content	Tone	Audience
17 Months						
Thurs Aug 06, 2015	46	Media Statement by MAS	02:00	Confirmation that flaperon was from MH370 / Families already informed and "extend our deepest sympathies to those affected" / Reiterate its cooperation with relevant authorities and continued communication with the families	Factual / Empathetic (English Only)	Media / General / Families
2 Years						
Tue Mar 08, 2016	47	Media Statement by MAS	16:15	MAS (administrator appointed) and MAB (new airline) held memorial service attended by employees and families of 13 staff – MAS reiterated commitment to Next of Kins	Factual / (English Only)	Media / General / Families (Last statement to date on MAS linked website)

* Both Kuala Lumpur and Beijing are GMT +8.

Table A4.4 Malaysian Government Media Statements April 8, 2014–August 28, 2014. (Malaysia Airlines MH370, 2019)

Date	Statement Number and source	When to say it? * (GMT +8)	What to say?	How to say it?	Who to say it to?
DAY 9					
Sun Mar 16, 2014	48 Press Briefing by Minister of Defense and Acting Minister of Transport	17:30	Response to a number of key enquiries and opening admission that every day brings new angles, and this information needs to be verified before it can be released – asks for patience / Covers search area update / Police investigation into passengers / Crew both air and ground / Visited pilots homes / Aircraft maintenance – aircraft was fit to fly / New IMMARSAT team	Factual (English only)	Media / General
DAY 10					
Mon Mar 17, 2014	49 Press Briefing by Minister of Defense and Acting Minister of Transport	17:30	Brief statement and operational update / Diplomatic efforts along the search corridors and also with countries with expertise / 26 countries now involved / Expert involvement / Police investigation / Malaysia's response – corroboration of information / Malaysia Airlines actions – focused on family assistance	Factual / Empathetic (Bi-lingual)	Media

DAY	Date	No.	Event	Time	Details		Audience

DAY 11

| Tues Mar 18, 2014 | 50 | MH370 Press Conference Transcript (Joint by MAS and Malaysian Govt.) | 17:30 | Search for MH370 has entered a new phase – international dimension / Updates on the northern and southern corridors and assets deployed / Malaysia Airlines updates the details about the ACARS and Transponder being switched off / No comment on the police investigation / Thanks to international community and reiterate that thoughts with the families and friends of those on board | Factual (Bi-lingual) | Media |

DAY 12

| Wed Mar 19, 2014 | 51 | Press Briefing by Minister of Defense and Acting Minister of Transport | 17:30 | Operational update / International search and rescue effort to narrow the corridors / Ministry of Foreign Affairs, Armed Forces and Dept. of Civil Aviation all involved / Clearing up way point rumour / police investigation update / High-level team to Beijing | Factual (Bi-lingual) | Media / General |

DAY 13

| Thurs Mar 20, 2014 | 52 | Press Briefing by Minister of Defense and Acting Minister of Transport | 17:30 | Update on Australian satellite images / Details on search efforts including numbers of craft deployed and countries involved / Update of care of families and focus on locating MH370 | Factual (English only) | Media / General |

(Continued)

Table A4.4 Continued

Date	Statement Number and source	When to say it? * (GMT +8)	What to say?	How to say it?	Who to say it to?
DAY 14					
Fri Mar 21, 2014	53 Press Briefing by Minister of Defense and Acting Minister of Transport	17:30	Operational update on Search efforts/ Satellite data processing procedures and timelines / Family briefing information	Factual (English only)	Media / General
DAY 15					
Sat Mar 22, 2014	54 Press Briefing by Minister of Defense and Acting Minister of Transport	17:59	Operational update: northern corridor no sightings of MH370 / Update on southern corridor and Australian search area / Kuala Lumpur briefing went well but not so in Beijing / Acknowledgement that Chinese briefings need to be improved – no blame / Transcript / Cargo manifest	Factual (Bi-lingual)	Media / General
DAY 16					
Sun Mar 23, 2014	55 Press Briefing by Minister of Defense and Acting Minister of Transport	18:00	Operational update / Family briefing in Beijing lasted six hours / ACARS transmission cleared	Factual (Bi-lingual)	Media / General
DAY 17					
Mon Mar 24, 2014	56 Press Briefing by Minister of Defense and Acting Minister of Transport	17:30	Operational update / Satellite images / Family briefings in Beijing lasted 8 hours, after more than 12 hours of meetings team has returned to Kuala Lumpur to discuss matters raised at the meetings and return to Beijing tomorrow / Police investigation update	Factual (English only)	Media

DAY 18

Date	No.	Event	Time	Content	Type	Audience
Tues Mar 25, 2014	57	Press Briefing by Minister of Defense and Acting Minister of Transport	18:50	Details on how the conclusion that MH370 ended in the Southern Indian Ocean was reached / Technical information / Search update	Factual (English only)	Media / General

DAY 19

Date	No.	Event	Time	Content	Type	Audience
Wed Mar 26, 2014	58	Press Briefing by Minister of Defense and Acting Minister of Transport	17:45	Operational updates / New satellite images / Assets deployed in search area / Chinese special envoy / International working group / Malaysia Airlines taking the lead on communicating with the families	Factual (English only)	Media / General

DAY 20

Date	No.	Event	Time	Content	Type	Audience
Thurs Mar 27, 2014	59	Press Briefing by Minister of Defense and Acting Minister of Transport	17:45	Updates: Chinese special envoy / Family briefing in Beijing / Working hard to make these briefings more productive / Search update assets deployed / Malaysian team going to Perth	Factual (English only)	Media / General

DAY 21

Date	No.	Event	Time	Content	Type	Audience
Fri Mar 28, 2014	60	Press Briefing by Minister of Defense and Acting Minister of Transport	17:45	Update: refined search area / New satellite images	Factual (English only)	Media / General

(Continued)

Table A4.4 Continued

Date	Statement Number and source	When to say it? * (GMT +8)	What to say?	How to say it?	Who to say it to?
DAY 24					
Mon Mar 31, 2014	61 Press Briefing by Minister of Defense and Acting Minister of Transport	18:15	PM visit to Perth / New Joint Agency Co-ordination Centre (JACC) set up in Perth / ASEAN defence meeting / Indonesian assistance / Next of kin flown to Kuala Lumpur for briefings from experts – broadcast live to other families in Beijing / Families want to know where is MH370 – we don't have the answer to this question	Factual Empathetic (English Only)	Media / General
DAY 25					
Tues Apr 01, 2014	62 Press Briefing by Minister of Defense and Acting Minister of Transport	17:45	Closed door briefing for families in Kuala Lumpur / Release of transcript	Factual (English Only)	Media / General
DAY 27					
Thurs Apr 03, 2014	63 Press Briefing by PM of Malaysia	12:00	PM thanking Australia during his visit to meet the search teams / Promise that they will not give up trying to find the plane	Empathetic (English Only)	Media / General / Families

DAY 29

Sat Apr 05, 2014	64 Press Briefing by Minister of Defense and Acting Minister of Transport	18:06	Almost a month since MH370 went missing / formation of three groups to continue investigation / three ministerial committees – including a next of kin committee / ASEAN update / Refuting allegations that Malaysia was complicit in what happened to MH370 – this should be above politics	Factual (English Only)	Media / General

DAY 31

Mon Apr 07, 2014	65 Press Briefing by Minister of Defense and Acting Minister of Transport	19:45	31 days post-disappearance / Update: Ping detection / Reiterate Govt. Committees	Factual (English Only)	Media / General

DAY 39

Tues Apr 15, 2014	66 Press Briefing by Minister of Defense and Acting Minister of Transport	15:15	New phase of search – details of this / Government set up international investigation team – not to blame or investigate criminal aspects but for ICAO recommendations from incident / Update on Committees	Factual (English Only)	Media / General

(Continued)

Table A4.4 Continued

Date	Statement Number and source	When to say it?* (GMT +8)	What to say?	How to say it?	Who to say it to?
DAY 43					
Sat Apr 19, 2014	67 Press Briefing by Minister of Defense and Acting Minister of Transport	14:30	Search becoming more difficult / Reiterating all possible effort made to recover MH370 / Search will not be abandoned but take a different approach / Mention of kin committee – particular mention of next of kin committee meeting with counterparts in Beijing	Factual (English Only)	Media / General
DAY 44					
Sun Apr 20, 2014	68 Press Briefing by Minister of Foreign Affairs and Chair of Next of Kin Committee	16:00	Opens with unprecedented situation / has chaired 3 next of kin meetings with reps from 16 ministries and agencies / morning meeting with families in Malaysia – dedicated representative assigned to discuss with Chinese Government's issues for Chinese next of kin / Flying to Beijing as Deputy Foreign Minister to firm up bi-lateral relations / Acknowledged the families want answers and touched on financial assistance	Factual / Empathetic (English Only)	Media / General
Day 73					
Mon May 19, 2014	69 Press Statement by Minister of Defense and Acting Minister of Transport	22:00	Update on search – Malaysia, Australia and China represented / Demands by next of kin for raw Inmarsat data – being discussed with Inmarsat for its release in interest of 'greater transparency'	Factual (English Only)	Media / General

Day 74				
Tues May 20, 2014	70 Inmarsat and Malaysian DCA Joint Press Statement	10:00	Commitment to release the Inmarsat data with a relevant explanation to enable the reader to understand the data / Stress that this data is just one element of the investigation	Factual (English Only)	Media / General
DAY 89				
Wed Jun 04, 2014	71 Press Statement by Minister of Defense and Acting Minister of Transport	19:00	Met with four Ministerial Committees / Continued and intensified search part of May 5th agreement between Malaysia, Australia and China / China and Malaysia continued commitment on 40th anniversary of diplomatic relations / Next of kin – reiterate commitment to them regardless of where they are / Tech Committee – details of data analysis progress / Update of Asset Deployment Committee – details / Communication, Coordination and Media Committee – working with reps from the other committees and will travel to Canberra first to get latest updates and then Beijing	Factual (English Only)	Media / General

(Continued)

Table A4.4 Continued

Date	Statement Number and source	When to say it? * (GMT +8)	What to say?	How to say it?	Who to say it to?
DAY 94					
Mon Jun 09, 2014	72 Briefing by Deputy Minister for Communications and Chair of the liaison, communication and Media Committee	16:00	Three months since MH370 missing – transition phase going well / Strengthen tripartite agreement and partners / Some details of trip to Canberra followed by trip to Beijing / Acknowledge Voice370 wish to meet Malaysia PM, Acting Transport Minister and Chair of next of kin Committee – arranging this in due time and establishing a working template dealing with issues raised by next of kin / Update on deployment and reiterate commitment to continue the search	Factual (English Only)	Media / General
DAY 121					
Sun Jul 06, 2014	73 Statement by Minister of Defense	13:38	Update on search and thanks to tripartite partners, Australia and China / Search continues to give closure to families of those on board MH370	Factual (English Only)	Media / General
Day 155					
Sat Aug 09, 2014	74 Statement by Minister of Transport	15:44	Five months of searching assure next of kin they remain committed / Aug 6th contracted search to Fugro – details of this plus additional measures	Factual (English Only)	Media / General

Day 166					
Wed Aug 20, 2014	75 Press Briefing by Minister of Defense	20:00	Opening paragraph empathetic and directed to next of kin / Cost sharing of search between Malaysia and Australia / Updates on deployments / Close with a personal message to next of kin regarding commitment to finding their loved ones	Factual / Empathetic (English Only)	Media / General / Families
DAY 174					
Thurs Aug 28, 2014	76 Tripartite Meeting Communique	13:15	Who attended meeting / Thanks and sympathies expressed for next of kin and commitment to find closure and understand the mystery / Detailed update of search	Factual (English Only)	Media / General
Thurs Aug 28, 2014	77 Statement sent on behalf of Minister of Transport / JACC Media	14:30	MOU signing for parameters of cooperation between Australia and Malaysia to continue the search for MH370 / Resolute effort to find aircraft and commitment to next of kin to find closure and regular updates includes JACC website details	Factual (English Only)	Media / General

* Both Kuala Lumpur and Beijing are GMT +8.

5 A new public relations crisis communication model

The discussion so far elucidates that an organisation has many publics and variable (sometimes transient) relationships with them. These relationships are realised via connections or communications that take place in the communication sphere which is a complex matrix of messages. It is essential to acknowledge that this complexity has been alluded to by the Social Mediated Crisis Communication Theory but it focuses on the nature of the relationship between the organisation and social and traditional media. Hvass (2014), on the other hand, highlights the direct and indirect relationships of offline word of mouth communication. Coombs (2007) also models the new communication space acknowledging the matrix of connections that now exist. However, the challenge lies in the simultaneous modelling of the organisation's relationships with their publics and the public's relationships with each other. Lastly, the complexity of relationships in the communication sphere is exacerbated by the very nature of the sphere itself.

The current communication scenario is illustrated in Figure 5.1. Here an organisation communicates directly with its publics (limited below to six as these are indicative only). These publics are also simultaneously connected in the communication sphere, communicating indirectly or directly with each other independent of the organisation. The model also represents the potential volume of content that is moving between publics; the difference in communication volume is also indicated. It is important to note that this model does not make any assumptions about the equity of the relationships and only acknowledges their existence.

The communication sphere is in crisis when an event damages the relationship between an organisation and its public threatening other existing relationships and sometimes the existence of the organisation as seen in Figure 5.2. The event triggers or creates a Public Relations Crisis, resulting in the deferment of normal communications and requiring an organisational crisis communication response.

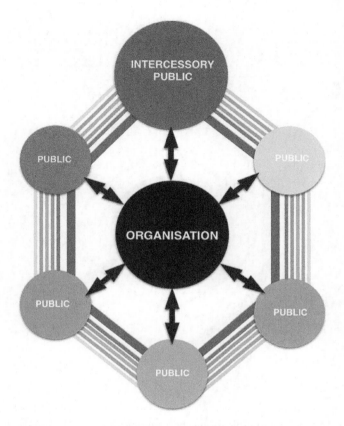

Figure 5.1 Non-crisis communication sphere model.

Based on the example of Malaysia Airlines MH370, Figure 5.3 indicates some of the key publics that are relevant in the aviation industry.

Both Benoit and Coombs advance public relations crisis communication theory, the former by identifying a typology of organisational responses and the latter by linking these responses to attributions of responsibility as defined by the event or situation. These two theorists contribute important tenets to improve public relations crisis communication but other dimensions need to be considered.

The public's attribution of responsibility is even more pressing in today's communication sphere. Now, intercessory publics, such as the media, have increasing access via online communication platforms (including social media) and are pressurised through their augmented

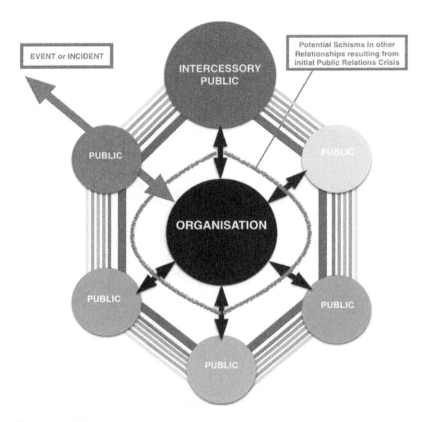

Figure 5.2 Crisis communication sphere model.

requirement for content to seek information and responses from those publics involved in or affected by an event.

The Vanishing of Flight MH370: The True Story of the Hunt for the Missing Malaysian Plane by Richard Quest, CNN's aviation expert highlights the above. In his 2016 book, Quest mentions the informed decision of CNN management to focus on the MH370 story and to investigate it in depth. Interestingly, Richard Quest's expertise on the topic can be attributed to a fortuitous interview with the first officer of MH370 for a travel show only two weeks prior to the event. Quest subsequently went from Asian to Aviation correspondent for CNN in a matter of weeks (Irving, 2016). New information attempting to unravel the aviation mystery appears in both traditional and social media periodically.

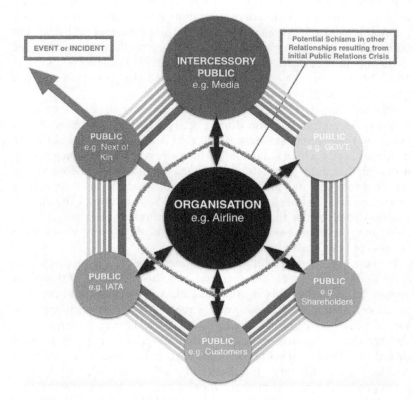

Figure 5.3 Aviation (MH370) crisis communication sphere model.

Accepting this emerging communication sphere, this new status quo, organisations need an added dimension to their crisis communication plans and strategies. There needs to be an additional facet to crisis communication theory, which is the creation of a hierarchy of crisis publics based on an assessment of publics according to both the event itself (Coombs's Situational Crisis Communication Theory) and the publics' proximity to the event, scaled against their varying attributions of responsibility.

The publics who have severed or damaged their relationship with the organisation as the result of an event are usually those publics who are the most affected by an event, and they will hold the highest attribution of responsibility. Therefore they need to be the first to be addressed in the organisation's crisis communication strategic response. Further, this response needs to correlate with the attributions of responsibility for it to be effective. In the current communication sphere, intercessory publics must also be given priority as they are powerful originators of communication during a crisis. Intercessory publics are not limited to the media. They can also include social media influencers, bloggers and others who are key communicators with an organisation's publics outside of their direct control.

Stephens et al. (2005, p. 394) allude to this in their work on stakeholder communication during crisis, highlighting observations made by Pfeffer and Salancik (1978) that organisations should make decisions about which stakeholders to address and which they can ignore. Further, they correctly assert that a public can be inconsequential or minor one day and of utmost importance the next depending on the event. What needs to be ascertained is how to rank the publics and how to prioritise them in terms of communication strategies. The consistency of crisis communication in terms of tailoring messages to various publics is also important.

In their work Stephens et al. (2005) note there is little research concerning how messages are targeted towards different stakeholder groups and whether this is even possible without eroding organisational credibility. If different publics require different responses and yet, as universally argued, organisational consistency is paramount, an organisation's crisis response communication strategy is doomed to fail. It is essential to tailor organisational responses to different publics (or stakeholders), and this can be achieved while maintaining consistency. The new communication sphere allows an organisation to achieve message tailoring and maintain consistency. Finally, of particular relevance to aviation is the likelihood of multiple contributing factors involved in an air event that reveal opportunities to an organisation for tailoring messages to specific publics without risking accusations of inconsistency.

From this case study it is clear that Malaysia Airlines did not effectively tailor their response to various publics and therefore did not meet their expectations, regardless of their ability to nominate them as priority publics, and this was a key factor in the flak faced by the airline.

An extension to the current theoretical model for public relations crisis communication is necessary. It would be beneficial to create a hierarchy of crisis publics based on their differing attributions of responsibility determined by their proximity to the event and/or the severing of their relationship with the organisation as a result of the event. This addition accommodates the varying responses required by different publics during a crisis as well as allows for organisations to understand the expectations of varying publics. This facilitates the tailoring of their crisis communication response, thereby increasing the effectiveness of crisis communication.

Figure 5.3 clarifies that there is a need to prioritise the publics experiencing the relationship schism, as they are at the vanguard of the crisis and the impact is proportional. Identifying key publics of a crisis is not a new concept in crisis communication. Fearn-Banks (2011) states that a priority of a crisis communication plan is identifying a list of key publics. However, this is not enough to ensure successful crisis communication. The convergence of media and publics in the communication sphere necessitates a rationale for heirarchically organising publics during a crisis. This will ensure the organisation sends messages tailored to the needs of each public, thereby minimising miscommunication. There is universal agreement that not all publics are going to be of equal importance during a crisis. However, there will be multiple publics that need simultaneous prioritising. The unique relation between the public, the organisation and the event is an indicator of the type of response. Therefore developing a hierarchy of crisis publics is essential if crisis resolution is to be effective.

Conclusion

The need for an additional dimension to theory through the exploration of existing theory relevant to public relations crisis communication has been established. Exploring significant communication theories, public relations crisis theory and stakeholder theory pointed out that there is a lack of constructive discussion on the varying attributions of responsibility of publics and the ramifications of this for organisational crisis communication response. Effective crisis communication is the most important tool that an organisation experiencing a public relations crisis has at its disposal. Given that purpose of crisis communication is to move an organisation through crisis to a point where recovery can commence, its importance cannot be underestimated.

However, this is not the only missing dimension in crisis communication. Other recommendations raised in this book include the use of various communication channels during a crisis and determining their function and purpose in relation to crisis communication. Given the issues with Malaysia Airlines' use of short messaging service it must be deliberated if this channel is to be disregarded in a crisis or if regulations for its use need to be developed. Referred to in the work of Stephens et al. (2005) and Hvass (2014) and reminiscent of Marshall McLuhan's (1964) media ecology is the impact the medium of communication has on the message and the publics receiving it. While this question is relevant for all of the actors in the communication sphere during normal communications it is ever more crucial during crisis communication particularly in terms of the organisation and the publics they identify as having high attributions of responsibility. Therefore research into communication channel typology during crisis communications would be another worthwhile extension to existing theory.

There is also a need to develop an organisational typology based on the organisation's crisis communication strategies. An investigation of the effect of an organisation's intrinsic personality on its ability to communicate through crisis is also valuable in order to provide greater understanding of crisis communication.

A hierarchy of crisis publics offers a new method for categorising an organisation's publics during a crisis and is expected to provide an indication of effective crisis response strategies for the organisation.

While the results of the case study and analysis point to a disconnect between the ability of Malaysia Airlines to accurately determine their hierarchy of publics and correlating attributions of responsibility, it remains the first such exploration and therefore more research is required, both within aviation and across other industries to validate the theory extension.

Finally this is just an initial foray into the concept of a hierarchy of publics and the benefit it potentially offers both the theory and practice of public relations crisis management. More research needs to be undertaken to determine the efficacy across differing industries and differing events since the ability of an organisation to control communication, particularly during a crisis, has diminished in recent times.

References

Anthonissen, Peter F, 2012, 'No Thrillers, But Hard Reality', in Anthonissen, Peter F (ed.), *Crisis Communications, Practical PR Strategies for Reputation Management and Company Survival*, Kogan Page Limited, Great Britain and United States, pp. 7–24.

Asia Pacific Accident Investigation Group (APAC-AIG/2), 2014, accessed on 29/2/2016, http://www.icao.int/Search/pages/Results.aspx?k=Amendment% 2014

Austin, L, Liu B F and Jin Y, 2012, 'How Audiences Seek Out Crisis Information: Exploring the Social-Mediated Crisis Communication Model', *Journal of Applied Communication Research*, Vol. 40, No. 2, pp. 188–207, doi: 10.1080/00909882.2012.654498

Balmer, John M T, Johansen T S and Nielsen, A E, 2016, 'Guest Editors' Introduction: Scrutinizing Stakeholder Thinking: Orthodoxy or Heterodoxy?' *International Studies of Management & Organization*, Vol. 46, No. 4, pp. 205–215, accessed on 12/4/2016.

Benoit, W L, 1997, 'Image Repair Discourse and Crisis Communication', *Public Relations Review*, Vol. 23, No. 2, pp. 177–186.

Benoit, W and Pang A, 2008, 'Crisis Communication and Image Repair Discourse', in Hansen T L and Neff B (eds.), *Public Relations: From Theory to Practice*, Pearson Education, Inc., Boston, MA, pp. 244–261.

Bernays, E L, 1923, *Crystallizing Public Opinion*, Boni and Liveright, New York.

Botan, C H and Hazelton, V, 2006, 'Public Relations in a New Age', in Botan C and Hazelton V (eds.), *Public Relations Theory II*, Routledge, Canada, pp. 1–19.

Brown, Robert E, 2015, *The Public Relations of Everything, The Ancient, Modern and Postmodern Dramatic History of An Idea*, Routledge, Oxon and New York.

Bucy, E P and Holbert R L, 2011, *Sourcebook for Political Communication Research Methods, Measures, and Analytical Techniques*, 1st Edition, Routledge, New York.

Butterick, K, 2011, *Introducing Publics Relations Theory and Practice*, Sage Publications Ltd, London, p. 62.

Charmaz, K, 2006, *Constructing Grounded Theory: A Practical Guide through Qualitative Analysis*, Sage Publications, London.

ch-aviation, 2015, *Malaysia Airlines Leadership in Change Ahead of New-Co's Launch*, accessed on 29/2/2016, http://www.ch-aviation.com/portal/news/36556-malaysia-airlines-leadership-in-change-ahead-of-newcos-launch

Coombs, W Timothy, 2006, 'Crisis Management: A Communicative Approach', in Botan C and Hazelton V (eds.), *Public Relations Theory II*, Routledge, Canada, pp. 171–198.

Coombs, W Timothy and Holladay, Sherry J, 2007, *It's not Just PR: Public Relations in Society*, Blackwell Publishing, United States, United Kingdom and Australia.

Coombs, W Timothy, 2007, 'Protecting Organization Reputations during a Crisis: The Development and Application of Situational Crisis Communication Theory', *Corporate Reputation Review*, Vol. 10, No. 3, pp. 163–177.

Coombs, W Timothy, 2012, 'Parameters for Crisis Communication', in Coombs, W Timothy and Holladay, Sherry J (eds.), *The Handbook of Crisis Communication*, Blackwell Publishing Ltd, United Kingdom, pp. 17–54.

Coombs, W Timothy and Holladay, S J, 2012, 'The Paracrisis: The Challenges Created by Publicity Managing Crisis Prevention', *Public Relations Review*, Vol. 38, No. 3, pp. 408–415.

Coombs, W Timothy and Holladay S J, 2014, 'How Publics React to Crisis Communication Efforts', *Journal of Communication Management*, Vol. 18, No. 1, pp. 40–57, accessed on 4/11/2015, doi:10.1108/JCOM-03-2013-0015

Deetz, S A, 1992, *Democracy in an Age of Corporate Colonization: Developments in Communication and the Politics of Everyday Life*, SUNY, United States.

Durham, M G and Kellner, D M, 2006, Editors, *Media and Cultural Studies*, Blackwell and Malden, MA.

Eisenhardt, Kathleen M, 1989, 'Building Theories from Case Study Research', *The Academy of Management Review*, Vol. 14, No.4, pp. 532–550, accessed on 1/3/2016.

Faulkner, B, 2001, 'Towards a Framework for Tourism Disaster Management', *Tourism Management*, Vol. 22, No.2, pp. 135–147.

Fearn-Banks, K, 2011, *Crisis Communications, A Casebook Approach*, 4th Edition, Routledge, New York.

Frandsen, F, and Johansen, W, 2007, 'Crisis Communication and the Rhetorical Arena: A Multivocal Approach', Conference Papers — International Communication Association, p. 1, *Communication & Mass Media Complete*, EBSCOhost, accessed on 15/11/2015.

Frandsen F and Johansen W, 2011, 'The Study of Internal Crisis Communication: Towards an Integrative Framework', *Corporate Communications: An International Journal*, Vol. 16 No. 4, pp. 347–361, accessed on 20/11/2015, doi:10.1108/13563281111186977

Friedman, Andrew L and Miles S, 2006, *Stakeholders*, Oxford University Press, Oxford, accessed on 12/04/2016, http://site.ebrary.com.ezproxy.uow.edu.au/lib/uow/detail.action?docID=10271574

Friedman, J, 2013, 'Milton Friedman was Wrong about Corporate Social Responsibility', weblog, accessed on 12/04/2016, http://www.huffington post.com/john-friedman/milton-friedman-was-wrong_b_3417866.html

Gonçalves, G, 2014, 'Political Public Relations: Origins, Challenges and Applications', *Comunicação e Sociedade*, Vol. 26, No. 2014, pp. 99–107.

Gordon A, 2011, *Public Relations*, Oxford University Press, New York.

Green A, 2010, *Creativity in Public Relations*, 4th Edition, Kogan Page Limited, United Kingdom and United States of America, p. 134.

Gregory, A, 2012, 'Public Relations and Management', in Theaker A (ed.), *The Public Relations Handbook*, 4th Edition, Routledge, Canada 2012, p. 69.

Griffin, E, 2012, *A First Look at Communication Theory*, 8th Edition, McGraw-Hill, New York.

Griffin A, 2014, *Crisis, Issues and Reputation Management*, Kogan Page Limited, United Kingdom and United States of America.

Grunig, J E, 2009, 'Paradigms of Global Relations in an Age of Digitalisation', *Prism* Vol. 6, No. 2, pp. 1–19.

Hall, https://www.spps.org/cms/lib/MN01910242/Centricity/Domain/125/iceberg_model_3.pdf

Hearit K M, 1995, '"Mistakes Were Made": Organizations, Apologia, and Crises of Social Legitimacy', *Communication Studies*, Vol. 46, No. 1–2, pp. 1–17, doi:10.1080/10510979509368435.

Heath, Robert L, 2012, 'Introduction', in Coombs, W Timothy and Holladay, Sherry J (eds.), *The Handbook of Crisis Communication*, Blackwell Publishing Ltd, United Kingdom, pp. 1–15.

Hendin J, Pendas de Cassina S and Walsh, J, 2008, 'Calamites', 'No Thrillers, But Hard Reality', in Anthonissen, Peter F (ed.), *Crisis Communications, Practical PR Strategies for Reputation Management and Company Survival*, Kogan Page Limited, Great Britain and United States, pp. 55–72.

Hurn, B and Tomalin, B, 2013, *Cross-Cultural Communication, Theory and Practice*, Palgrave MacMillan, United Kingdom.

Hvass, K A, 2014, 'Tourism Social Media and Crisis Communication: An Erupting Trend', *Tourism Social Media: Transformations in Identity, Community and Culture*. Published online: 11 Sep 2014; 177–191, accessed on 29/02/2016, doi:10.1108/S1571-5043(2013)0000018012

Iacono, J C, Brown, A and Holtham, C, 2011, 'The Use of the Case Study Method in Theory Testing: The Example of Steel eMarketplaces', *The Electronic Journal of Business Research Methods*, Vol. 9, No. 1, pp. 57–65

IATA n.d., accessed on 29/2/2016, http://www.iata.org/about/pages/index.aspx

ICAO n.d., accessed on 29/2/2016, http://www.icao.int/about-icao/Pages/default.aspx

ICAO, 2013, *Safety Management Manual*, 3rd Edition, accessed on 29/2/2016, http://www.icao.int/safety/SafetyManagement/Documents/Doc.9859.3rd%20Edition.alltext.en.pdf

Irving, C, 2016, 'The Secret of CNN's Turnaround: Flight MH370', The Dailybeast, 03.06.16 9:15 AM ET, accessed on 29/2/2016.

Kruckeberg, D, 1998, 'The Future of PR Education: Some Recommendations', *Public Relations Review*, Vol. 24, No. 2, pp. 235–248.

Leetaru, K, 2016, 'Mapping World Happiness and Conflict through Global News and Image Mining', available at: https://www.forbes.com/sites/ka levleetaru/2016/01/13/mapping-world-happiness-and-conflict-through-global-news-and-image-mining/#22d00e8ee224, accessed on 23/6/2019.

Leitch, S, and Neilson, D, 2001, 'Bringing Publics into Public Relations: New Theoretical Frameworks for Practice', in Heath R L (ed.), *Handbook of Public Relations*, Sage, Thousand Oaks, CA, pp. 127–138.

Leithead, A, 2014, *'Malaysia Airlines CEO: 'We're Not Hiding Anything'',* *BBC News*, accessed on 29/2/2016, https://www.youtube.com/watch?v=ilf3 we0Fbz4

Liu, B F, Austin, L and Jin, Y, 2011, 'How Publics Respond to Crisis Communication Strategies: The Interplay of Information Form and Source', *Public Relations Review*, Vol. 37, pp. 345–353.

Maditinos, Z and Vassiliadis, C, 2008, Crises and Disasters in Tourism Industry: Happen Locally - Affect Globally, p. 69, http://mibes.teilar.gr/ebook/ ebooks/ maditinos_vasiliadis%2067–76.pdf, accessed on 20/11/2015.

Malaysia Airlines MH17, 2019, accessed on 2/7/2019, http://www.malaysiaairlines.com/my/en/site/mh17.html

Malaysia Airlines MH370, 2019, accessed on 2/7/2019, http://www.malaysia airlines.com/my/en/site/mh370.html

Marr, B, 2018, 'How Much Data Do We Create Every Day? The Mind-Blowing Stats Everyone Should Read', available at: https://www.forbes.com/sites/ bernardmarr/2018/05/21/how-much-data-do-we-create-every-day-the-mind-blowing-stats-everyone-should-read/#2804a67460ba, accessed on 21/6/2019.

McLuhan, M, 1964, *Understanding Media: Extensions of Man*, Mentor, New York, NY, USA.

Mcquail, D and Windahl, D S, 2015, *Communication Models for the Study of Mass Communications*, Routledge, United Kingdom.

Murphy, P, 1996, 'Chaos Theory as a Model for Managing Issues and Crises', *Public Relations Review*, Vol. 22, No. 2, pp. 95–113.

Norton C, 2013, 'Online Crisis Management', in Brown R and Waddington S (eds.), *Share This Too, More Social Media Solutions For PR Professionals*, John Wiley & Sons, United Kingdom, pp. 159–169.

Oliveira M, 2013, 'Multicultural Environments and Their Challenges to Crisis Communication', *Journal of Business Communication*, Vol. 50, No. 3, pp. 253–277, accessed on 20/11/2015.

Pang A, Abul Hassan, N B and and ChongPang, A, 2013, 'Negotiating Crisis in the Social Media Environment, Evolution of Crises Online, Gaining Credibility Offline', *Corporate Communications: An International Journal*, Vol. 19, No. 1, pp. 96–118, accessed on 20/11/2015.

Pearson C, Clair J, Misra, S and Mitroff, I, 1997 (Autumn), 'Managing the Unthinkable', *Organizational Dynamics*, Vol. 26, No. 2, p. 51, accessed on 20/11/2015.

Pfau, M and Wan H, 2006, 'Persuasion: An Intrinsic Function of Public Relations', in Botan C and Hazelton V (eds.), *Public Relations Theory II*, Routledge, Canada, pp. 101–136.

Phillips, D and Young, P, 2009, *Online Public Relations: A Practical Guide to Developing an Online Strategy in the World of Social Media*, Kogan Page Publishers, United Kingdom.

PRSA, 2019, 'About Public Relations', available at: https://www.prsa.org/all-about-pr/, accessed 3 June 2019.

Ralph, N, Birks, M and Chapman, Y, 2014, 'Contextual Positioning: Using Documents as Extant Data in Grounded Theory Research,' SAGE Open, July-September 2014: 1–7, accessed on 1/3/2016.

Silvia T and Anzur T, 2011, *Power Performance: Multimedia Storytelling for Journalism and Publics relations*, 1st Edition, Blackwell Publishing, United Kingdom.

Skybrary.aero 2016, James Reason HF Model, viewed on 20/11/2015, http://www.skybrary.aero/index.php/James_Reason_HF_Model.

Smith, R D, 2013, *Strategic Planning for Public Relations*, 4th Edition, Routledge, New York.

Sriramesh, K, 2009, *The Relationship between Culture and Public Relations from: The Global Public Relations Handbook, Theory, Research, and Practice*, Routledge, New York, accessed on: 22/7/2019.

Stacy, R N, 2013, 'Stakeholder Theory', Salem Press Encyclopedia, Research Starters, EBSCOhost, accessed on 12/04/2016.

Stephens, Keri K, Malone, Patty Callish and Bailey, Christine M, 2005, 'Communicating With Stakeholders During a Crisis, Evaluating Message Strategies', *Journal of Business Communication*, Vol. 42, No. 4, pp. 390–419, accessed on 12/04/2016, http://job.sagepub.com.ezproxy.uow.edu.au/content/42/4/390.full.pdf+html

Subramaniam, P, 2014, 'Finance Ministry Tables Bill on Takeover, Re-branding of Ailing MAS', Malaymail Online, Wednesday November 26, 2014, 01:15 PM GMT+8, accessed on accessed on 29/2/2016, http://www.themalaymailonline.com/malaysia/article/finance-ministry-tables-bill-on-takeover-rebranding-of-ailing-mas

Taylor, A, 2014, 'Bhopal: The World's Worst Industrial Disaster, 30 Years Later', available at: https://www.theatlantic.com/photo/2014/12/bhopal-the-worlds-worst-industrial-disaster-30-years-later/100864/, accessed on 24/7/2019.

Thomas, M, 2015, 'Flying Lessons: Malaysia and Other Airlines Avoiding Pan Am's Final Destination', *Strategic Direction*, Vol. 31, No. 8, pp. 26–28, accessed on 29/2/2016.

Topham, G, 2015, 'Malaysia Airlines 'technically bankrupt' as New Chief Seeks to Shed 6,000 Jobs, Christoph Mueller Remains Optimistic Carrier Can Regain Leading Regional Role Despite Financial Troubles and Legacy of MH370 and MH17 Disasters', *The Guardian*, Monday 1 June 2015 18.04 BST, accessed on 29/2/2016, https://www.theguardian.com/business/2015/jun/01/malaysia-airlines-technically- bankrupt-christoph-mueller-cuts-boss

Ulmer, Robert R, Sellnow, Timothy L and Seeger, Matthew W, 2015, *Effective Crisis Communication, Moving from Crisis to Opportunity*, SAGE Publications, United States.

World Internet Usage and Population Statistics, 2019, available at: https://www.internetworldstats.com/stats.htm, accessed on 2/8/2019.

Yin, Robert K, 2003, *Case Study Research Design and Methods*, 3rd Edition, Sage Publications, London.

Yin, Robert K, 2004, *The Case Study Anthology*, Sage Publications, London.

Young, A, 2019, TO70's Civil Aviation Safety Review 2018, accessed on 1/8/2019, https://to70.com/to70s-civil-aviation-safety-review-2018/.

Zimmer, S, 2015, 'Stakeholder Theory and Analysis', *Research Starters: Business* (Online Edition), Research Starters, EBSCO*host*, accessed on 12/04/2016.

Index

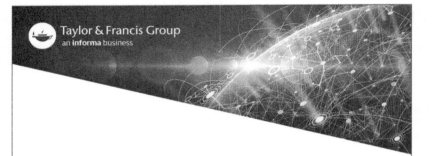